Gun Digest ® Handbook of

Collectible
American Guns

Ken Ramage

©2007 by
Krause Publications

Published by

Gun Digest Books
An imprint of F+W Publications
700 East State Street • Iola, WI 54990-0001
715-445-2214 • 888-457-2873
www.gundigestbooks.com

Our toll-free number to place an order or obtain
a free catalog is (800) 258-0929.

Library of Congress Control Number: 2006935651

ISBN 13: 978-0-89689-513-3
ISBN 10: 0-89689-513-0

Designed by Patsy Howell
Edited by Ken Ramage

Printed in China

Contents

Introduction

To many, the term "collectible" means antique. If firearms are the collectible category under discussion, then flintlocks and Civil War arms immediately come to mind. To others, "collectible" means high-end, limited production modern arms. Both are right.

There is, however, another class of collectible arms that includes certain makes and models of American-made firearms that were produced after 1900. Most, in fact, were produced from the 1920s to around 1940 (pre-war) and from 1946 to the 1960s (post-war) and some into the 1980s.

This post-1900 period may well be the golden age of American gunmaking. Our manufacturing capabilities in metal-cutting and wood-shaping had become fairly refined and the American sporting arms market was growing. Up through the post-war period, and beyond, many armsmakers relied upon skilled craftsmen to hand-fit the various parts needed to build a firearm. The gun steel received a high polish, and a deep blue finish. The wood stocks were machine-inlet, and cleaned up by hand. Early rifle stocks could be slender and graceful; the Savage Model 1999 is a good example, and the pre-64 Winchester Model 70 is another.

When asked to characterize this period, my most concise (and I think widely understandable) response to date has been to say the era is represented by the lifespan of the modern blued steel revolver from Smith & Wesson and Colt.

Why are these older modern firearms interesting? Craftsmanship. Compare a specimen from the pre/post-war era with a similar model of recent manufacture. Cycle the action, run your hands over the piece…you'll see and feel the difference. There are a great number of these well-made firearms out there, and often they do not command high prices. Many, in fact, are noticeably less expensive than a similar model fresh out of the box.

Firearms manufacturing is fundamentally the same as any other. Technological advances have made it possible—no, imperative—to rely upon increasingly sophisticated machines to perform all operations up to and, in some cases, including final finishing. Economics of the marketplace have made handwork increasingly expensive, and today computer-guided machines can pick up a piece of steel and carve a finished frame or receiver without human involvement. These machines even self-test their tooling dimensions and, if a tool goes out-of-spec, the machine stops the work-in-process, automatically changes out the bad part and resumes work in remarkably short order.

Blued steel requires skillful polishing and finishing. Stainless steel, on the other hand, proves less demanding. It has other advantages as well, rust-resistance being foremost. Also, modern stainless is easier to machine than was the early stainless thanks to improved formulas and greater knowledge of the necessary machining techniques. The latest major manufacturing innovation is the injection-molded polymer frame, which we see in more recent autoloading pistol designs, beginning with the Glock. Synthetic stocks and frames are not terribly new, and one of the models listed herein is mostly synthetic—the Remington Nylon 66 (and its relatives).

How to Use This Book

This book contains listings for several hundred firearms made by American gunmakers. These companies are arranged in alphabetical order, and each section includes a brief introduction, model specifications and prices. In some cases, closely related derivative models are also listed. Each model is valued at the three grades of condition in which it is commonly found, using the NRA Modern Condition Pricing Standards. These prices reflect high gun show/low gun shop retail pricing levels.

If you are selling the firearm directly to the next owner, these published prices indicate the zone of value appropriate for the model and condition. If, however, you are selling the gun to a gun dealer, or consigning it to an auction, be prepared to pocket substantially less than the listed prices. Why? Because the dealer will have to lay out his working capital for an unknown period of time, and ultimately make a reasonable profit. Consigning the gun to a dealer or an auction service can be an alternative. In both cases, the final selling price (never a certain thing) of the gun is reduced by the commission charged, which may run from 20 to 30 percent or more.

Determining Value

Demand and Availability

When demand exceeds availability, the price of the firearm will increase. For collectibles, although the supply is fixed, demand plays a similar role in establishing value. Some older firearms may be in scarce supply, yet are not in demand by collectors. Without demand, regardless of availability, the dollar value of the firearm will be lower.

Condition

Condition is arguably the most important factor in determining value by both shooters and collectors. All else being equal, the high-condition (NRA New/Perfect) specimen will bring substantially more money than will a gun that is rated NRA Good.

Collectors and shooters often differ in applying the NRA's condition criteria to even the same firearm. The collector is happiest with a nice exterior on a model he needs for his collection, even if the bore is badly pitted. The shooter appreciates the exterior as well, but places his emphasis on the interior condition of the bore and functionality of the action and magazine. The collector might rate this gun as Excellent, and the shooter would likely rate it only as Fair.

Pricing

Pricing, like condition, can be highly subjective. Regional interests and the time of year also play a role when calculating a realistic value for a given firearm. It is important to remember that published price references, like this book, are really only guidelines, not carved-in-stone firm pricing references. Ultimately, any firearm is worth only what you can get for it.

NRA Modern Arms Condition Standards

We have made slight elaborations *(in italics)* to the NRA standards to help readers determine degrees of condition.

- **New:** In the same condition as current factory production, *with original box and accessories.*
- **Perfect:** In new condition in every respect, *but may be lacking box and/or accessories.*
- **Excellent:** *Near* new condition, used but little, no noticeable marring of wood or metal, bluing perfect (except at muzzle or sharp edges).
- **Very Good:** In perfect working condition, no appreciable wear on working surfaces, *visible finish wear* but no corrosion or pitting, only minor surface dents or scratches.
- **Good:** In safe working condition, minor wear on working surfaces, no corrosion or pitting that will interfere with proper functioning.
- **Fair:** In safe working condition, but well worn, perhaps requiring replacement of minor parts or adjustments, no rust, but may have corrosion pits which do not render article unsafe or inoperable.

Acknowledgments

A book of this nature is seldom the work of a single person, and this book is no exception.

Photography of the listed guns came to me from a number of sources. Foremost are the photographs from noted firearms photographer Paul Goodwin. Also, my sincere thanks to Hunter Kirkland of Dixie Gunworks for his invaluable assistance in gathering photographs, and to other industry friends who pitched in to fill out the illustration needs: Tony Aeschliman, Marlin Firearms; Dwight van Brunt, Kimber, and Ken Jorgensen and Elaine Sandberg, Sturm, Ruger & Co., and Rock Island Auction Company.

Books on collectible arms (and other subjects) are of necessity works in progress. Your suggestions and constructive comments are welcome.

Ken Ramage
Iola, Wisconsin
February 2007

A.H. Fox

Philadelphia, Pennsylvania

The Fox Gun Company was established in Baltimore, Maryland, in 1896 by Ansley H. Fox. Early arms produced in his factory were made under the name of the Philadelphia Gun Company and 1905 he began operating under the name A.H. Fox. In 1930, this company was purchased by the Savage Arms Company, who continued manufacturing all grades of Fox shotguns. From 1942 onward, Savage made only the plainer grades of shotguns.

Paul Goodwin photo

A.H. FOX HAMMERLESS DOUBLE BARREL (1905-1946)

Side-by-side; boxlock; 12-, 16-, 20-ga.; 2$\frac{9}{16}$-inch (until mid-1930s), 2$\frac{3}{4}$-inch, 3-inch chambers; Krupp fluid steel (until about 1910), Chromox steel barrels (used exclusively after the early 1920s); walnut half-pistol-grip stock standard, straight or pistol grip optional; earliest graded smallbores have snap-on forend latch; standard engraving patterns for all grades except CE were changed 1913-1914; all graded 12-ga. and graded smallbores built after 1913 have Deeley finger-lever forend latch; Fox-Kautzky single trigger available in all grades after 1914; other options included beavertail forend, vent rib, skeleton steel butt, recoil pad, extra sets of barrels, custom stocks. 12-ga. introduced 1905; 16-, 20-ga. introduced 1912 and built on the same, scaled-down frame. Made by A.H. Fox Gun Company, Philadelphia, 1905-1929; taken over by Savage Arms Company in late 1929 and production moved to Utica, New York in 1930; production of the original A.H. Fox gun discontinued in 1946. Approximate production totals: graded 12-ga., 35,000; graded 16-ga., 3521; graded 20-ga., 3434.

A.H. FOX HAMMERLESS DOUBLE BARREL *(cont.)*

Double Barrel A Grade
Same specs as Hammerless Double Barrel (1905-1946) except 26-inch to 32-inch barrels; American walnut stocks; double or single trigger; extractors. Introduced 1905; discontinued 1942.

    Exc.: $1400   **VGood:** $950   **Good:** $800

A.H. Fox Hammerless Double Barrel AE Grade
Same specs as Hammerless Double Barrel (1905-1946) except 26-inch to 32-inch barrels; American walnut stocks; double or single trigger; ejectors. Introduced 1905; discontinued 1946.

    Exc.: $1600   **VGood:** $1150   **Good:** $950

A.H. Fox Hammerless Double Barrel CE Grade
Same specs as Hammerless Double Barrel (1905-1946) except 26-inch to 32-inch barrels; English walnut stocks; double or single trigger; ejectors. Introduced 1905; discontinued 1946.

    Exc.: $3800   **VGood:** $3100   **Good:** $2600

A.H. Fox Hammerless Double Barrel DE Grade
Same specs as Hammerless Double Barrel (1905-1946) except 26-inch to 32-inch barrels; Circassian walnut stocks; double or single trigger; ejectors. Introduced 1905; discontinued 1945.

    Exc.: $8000   **VGood:** $6000   **Good:** $4500

A.H. Fox Hammerless Double Barrel FE Grade
Same specs as Hammerless Double Barrel (1905-1946) except 26-inch to 32-inch barrels; Circassian walnut stocks; ejectors; made to order with any available option at no extra charge. Introduced 1906; discontinued 1940.

    Exc.: $16,500   **VGood:** $12,000   **Good:** $10,000

A.H. Fox Hammerless Double Barrel XE Grade
Same specs as Hammerless Double Barrel (1905-1946) except 26-inch to 32-inch barrels; Circassian walnut stocks; Monte Carlo comb optional; double or single trigger; ejectors. Introduced 1914; discontinued 1945.

    Exc.: $5750   **VGood:** $4800   **Good:** $3800

Paul Goodwin photo

A.H. FOX STERLINGWORTH

Side-by-side; boxlock; 12-, 16-, 20-ga.; 2⁹⁄₁₆-inch (until mid-1930s), 2¾-inch, 3-inch chambers; 26-inch to 32-inch Krupp fluid steel (until about 1910), Chromox steel barrels (used exclusively after the early 1920s); checkered American walnut half-pistol-grip stock, snap-on forend standard; straight or pistol grip optional; snap-on forend latch; double triggers; optional Fox-Kautzky single trigger available in all grades after 1914; extractors; standard engraving patterns for all grades except CE were changed 1913-1914; other options include beavertail forend, vent rib, skeleton steel butt, recoil pad, extra sets of barrels, custom stocks; mechanically same as other A.H. Fox doubles, but purely production-line guns without much handwork. Introduced 1911; discontinued 1946. Made by A.H. Fox Gun Company, Philadelphia, 1905-1929; taken over by Savage Arms Company in late 1929 and production moved to Utica, New York in 1930; production of the original A.H. Fox gun discontinued in 1946. Approximate production totals: 12-ga. Sterlingworth, 110,000; Sterlingworth 16-ga., 28,000; 20-ga. Sterlingworth, 21,000.

> **Exc.:** $1000 **VGood:** $700 **Good:** $450

A.H. Fox Sterlingworth Brush

Same specs as Fox Sterlingworth except 26-inch Cylinder/Modified barrels. Introduced 1911; discontinued 1930.

> **Exc.:** $1000 **VGood:** $700 **Good:** $450

A.H. Fox Sterlingworth Ejector

Same specs as Fox Sterlingworth except ejectors. Introduced 1911; discontinued 1946.

> **Exc.:** $1200 **VGood:** $900 **Good:** $650

A.H. Fox Sterlingworth Field

Same specs as Fox Sterlingworth except 28-inch Modified/Full barrels. Introduced 1911; discontinued 1930.

> **Exc.:** $1000 **VGood:** $700 **Good:** $450

A.H. Fox Sterlingworth Standard

Same specs as Fox Sterlingworth except 30-inch Full/Full barrels. Introduced 1911; discontinued 1930.

> **Exc.:** $1000 **VGood:** $700 **Good:** $450

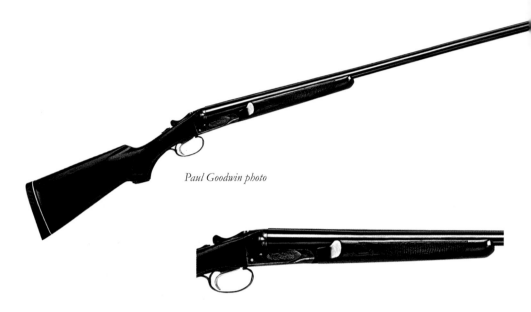

Paul Goodwin photo

A.H. FOX MODEL B LIGHTWEIGHT

Side-by-side; boxlock; hammerless; 12-, 20-ga., .410; 24-inch Improved/Modified (12-, 20-ga. only), 26-inch Full/Full (.410 only), 26-inch Improved/Modified, 28-inch Modified/Full, 30-inch Modified/Full (12-ga. only) barrels; vent rib; checkered select walnut pistol-grip stock, beavertail forearm; double triggers; color case-hardened frame. Introduced 1973; no longer in production.

Perf.: $150   **Exc.:** $120   **VGood:** $100

AMT

AMT / Crusader Arms
5200 Mitchelldale, Ste. E17
Houston, TX 77092
Phone: *800-272-7816*
Website: *www.highstandard.com*

This U.S. manufacturer has been through a lot of changes since its inception as Arcadia Machine & Tool Irwindale Arms in the 1980s. The business remained in Irwindale, California until it was acquired by Galena Industries and moved to Sturgis, South Dakota in late 1998/early 1999. Unfortunately the Galena ownership could not make a go of it and folded in 2001.

It appeared AMT was gone for good until 2004, when the tooling was acquired by the Crusader Gun Company, Inc., which is a subsidiary of High Standard Mfg. Co. of the same address. Other businesses/brands (besides AMT) under the same corporate umbrella today include High Standard, Firearms International, U.S. Cartridge Company and International Armament Corporation.

Paul Goodwin photo

AMT AUTOMAG V

Semi-automatic; single action; 50 AE; 5-shot magazine; 6½-inch barrel; 10½-inch overall length; weighs 46 oz.; carbon fiber grips; blade front sight, adjustable rear; stainless steel construction with brushed finish. Made in U.S. by AMT. Introduced 1990; dropped 1995.

    Perf.: $815   **Exc.:** $700   **VGood:** $625

AUTOMAG

AMT / AutoMag
High Standard Manufacturing Company
5200 Mitchelldale, Ste. E17
Houston, TX 77092
Phone: *800-272-7816*
Website: *www.highstandard.com*

Now a brand offered by High Standard Manufacturing Company, the AutoMag offering presently consists of the Backup 380, Backup 45 (plus other chamberings) and the AutoMag II pistol. The AutoMag line came from the defunct Galena Industries, as did AMT.

This brand had its beginnings with the unique stainless steel autoloading pistol, chambered for a new cartridge – the 44 AMP (AutoMag Pistol), developed in the early '70s by the Sanford Arms Company of Pasadena, California. Subsequently the original pistol, and other models as developed, were manufactured by a series of companies, to include: AutoMag Corp. (Pasadena, Calif.), TDE Corp. (North Hollywood, Calif.), TDE Corp. (El Monte, Calif.), High Standard (Hamden, Conn.), TDE-OMC, AMT ("C" Series), L. E. Jurras Custom (custom maker of limited number in 1977), Kent Lomont (made prototypes) and, in 1998, Auto Mag Inc. (Irwindale, Calif.) made 1,000 units of the Harry Sanford Commemorative.

Total production of the AutoMag Pistol varies a bit depending upon the source, but the total appears to be between 7,000 and 10,000 units over the entire life of the gun.

Paul Goodwin photo

AUTOMAG

Semi-automatic; 357 AutoMag., 44 AutoMag.; 7-shot magazine; 6½-inch barrel; 11½-inch overall length; short recoil; rotary bolt system; stainless steel construction; checkered plastic grips; fully-adjustable rear sight, ramp front. Manufactured by Auto Mag. Corp. and TDE Corp. to 1982.

Original Pasadena manufacture
Perf.: $2500   **Exc.:** $2300   **VGood:** $1995

TDE North Hollywood marked
Perf.: $2275   **Exc.:** $1850   **VGood:** $1700

Did You Know?

Although few were built, the firearm gained some notoriety in Hollywood. The AutoMag was showcased in the fourth "Dirty Harry" movie, "Sudden Impact", starring Clint Eastwood as Harry Callahan.

AUTO-ORDNANCE
CORPORATION

A Division of Kahr Arms
One Blue Hill Plaza
Pearl River, New York 10965
Phone: *845-652-8535*
Website: *www.kahr.com*

In 1999 Auto-Ordnance was acquired by Kahr Arms, and the corporate offices relocated to Pearl River, New York. Previously the company was a division of The Gun Parts Corporation (formerly Numrich Arms).
The company manufactures a semi-automatic version of the 1927 Thompson sub-machinegun. Full-auto Thompsons were discontinued in 1986.

Paul Goodwin photo

AUTO-ORDNANCE 1927A3

Semi-automatic; 22 LR; 10-, 30- or 50-shot magazine; 16-inch finned barrel; weighs about 7 lbs; walnut stock and forend; blade front sight, open fully-adjustable rear; recreation of the Thompson Model 1927; alloy receiver. Made in U.S. by Auto-Ordnance. No longer produced.

    Perf.: $700   **Exc.:** $600   **VGood:** $400

CHARTER ARMS

Manufacturing:
273 Canal St., Shelton, CT 06484. **Phone:** *203-922-1652.*
Website: *www.charterfirearms.com*
Sales & Marketing:
MKS Supply, 8611-A North Dixie Drive, Dayton OH 45414.
Phone: *937-454-0363.* **Website:** *www.hi-pointfirearms.com*

Charter Arms was founded in 1964 to produce affordable, reliable handguns. The first pistol was a lightweight, five-shot revolver called "The Undercover," chambered for the 38 Special cartridge. The one-piece frame provided strength that allowed the new revolver to safely shoot hot loads. The number of moving parts was reduced and a firing pin safety device created.

A unique hammer block system gave gun owners protection against unintentional discharges. The Undercover became popular with gun enthusiasts and law enforcement officers and became the platform upon which a comprehensive line of firearms was built, including the 44 Bulldog. Soon, the lightweight 44 Bulldog gained fame as the most powerful snub-nosed handgun in existence.

The company went bankrupt in the 1990s, but the Charter design and mark was resurrected for the 21st century by Charter 2000. The new company capitalized on the old Charter Arms revolvers, which had fewer moving parts and a simpler, trouble-free design.

Basing their new line of weapons on the basic Charter Arms design, the new company made a few improvements, to include a one-piece barrel/front sight that was rifled with eight grooves instead of six. The new models feature a hammer-block safety system so the gun cannot fire unless the trigger is held fully to the rear.

In addition to reintroducing the 38 Special Undercover and the 44 Special Bulldog, Charter 2000 produces revolvers chambered for 22 Long Rifle/22 Magnum (the Pathfinder), 357 Magnum (the Mag Pug) and 38 Special (the Off-Duty and the Police Bulldog).

In 2005, Charter 2000 announced it would file for bankruptcy. In September 2005, MKS Supply entered into an agreement with Charter Arms where MKS Supply would handle the sales, marketing and distribution for Charter Arms. This arrangement continues to the present.

Paul Goodwin photo

CHARTER ARMS BULLDOG

Revolver; double action; 44 Spl.; 5-shot cylinder; 2½-inch, 3-inch barrel; 7½-inch overall length; weighs 19 oz.; square notch fixed rear sight, Patridge-type front; checkered walnut or neoprene grips; chrome-moly steel frame; wide trigger and hammer, or spurless pocket hammer; blued or stainless finish. Introduced 1973; dropped 1996. Currently produced by Charter 2000, Inc.

    Perf.: $255   **Exc.:** $185   **VGood:** $155

Stainless Bulldog (discontinued 1991)

    Perf.: $275   **Exc.:** $195   **VGood:** $165

Colt's Manufacturing Company, LLC

P.O. Box 1868
Hartford, CT 06144-1868
Phone: *860-236-6311*
Website: *www.coltsmfg.com*

Colt is arguably among the most globally recognized brands in existence. Colt revolvers armed the Texas Rangers in the mid-1850s. Colt revolvers served widely in the Civil War. Afterwards, the metallic cartridge was perfected and the Colt Single Action Army revolver was introduced. The rest is history.

Founded in 1836 to produce percussion revolvers designed by Sam Colt, such as the Paterson, the business encountered tough sledding and eventually folded. Later, in 1847, a new Colt company was formed to manufacture an improved revolver design and was successful. The rest of the century was good for Colt, and it got better in 1897 when the company concluded an agreement with John Browning that ultimately resulted in the most popular autoloading pistol design ever, the 45-caliber Colt Model 1911 Government autoloading pistol. This legendary pistol became the standard issue sidearm for the U.S. military from 1911 to the late 1980s…and it is still issued today to selected units.

The success of the Colt Model 1911 pistol in the military market was mirrored in the commercial market, and Colt prospered. New models of revolvers and autoloading pistols appeared and were successful. The venerable Single Action Army was the backbone of the company until the advent of the Model 1911, and even afterwards, in an increasingly modern world, the Colt SAA continued in production––with just a few interruptions—to the present day.

In more recent years, Colt fell on hard times. It was acquired by conglomerates that extracted as much as possible from the business, neglecting the long-term needs of innovation and product development. The high cost of operating in the Hartford area and a union labor force added to the strain, and the company found itself once again on the ropes. A change of ownership occurred. The net result was that Colt finally settled into a successful business model that emphasized the military and law enforcement markets, and deemphasized the commercial market. Numerous pistols and revolvers were discontinued, including the well-made Python that is often referred to as the Cadillac of revolvers.

Today there are two Colts. One is Colt Defense, which deals with the military and law enforcement products and markets. The other is Colt's Manufacturing Company, LLC, which produces and markets the rather short line of Model 1911s, the AR-15 target rifles and the only Colt revolver offered today, the Single Action Army.

COLT AUTOLOADING PISTOLS

Paul Goodwin photo

COLT WOODSMAN (First Issue)

Semi-automatic; 22 LR standard velocity; 10-shot magazine; 6½-inch barrel; 10½-inch overall length. Designation, "The Woodsman," added after serial number 34,000; adjustable sights; checkered walnut grips. Introduced 1915; replaced 1943. Collector value.

    Exc.: $1295   **VGood:** $995   **Good:** $650

Colt Woodsman (First Issue) Sport Model

Same specs as First Issue Woodsman except adjustable rear sight; adjustable or fixed front; 4½-inch barrel; 8½-inch overall length; fires standard- or high-velocity 22 LR ammo. Introduced 1933; dropped 1943.

    Exc.: $1295   **VGood:** $995   **Good:** $650

Courtesy Dixie Gunworks

COLT WOODSMAN MATCH TARGET (First Issue)

Same specs as Woodsman First Issue except 6½-inch flat-sided barrel; 11-inch overall length; adjustable rear sight, blade front; checkered walnut one-piece extension grips; blued. Introduced 1938; dropped 1943.

Exc.: $2495   **VGood:** $1895   **Good:** $1095

U.S. Property marked
Exc.: $2700   **VGood:** $2200   **Good:** $1500

Did You Know?

The elongated, one-piece wraparound walnut grips were nicknamed "Elephant Ears." Unfortunately, they were somewhat fragile and often broke. Many serious target shooters of the day replaced them, severely affecting the value of the gun.

Paul Goodwin photo

COLT WOODSMAN (Second Issue)

Semi-automatic; 22 LR; 10-shot magazine; 6½-inch barrel; 10½-inch overall length; slide stop; hold-open device; heat-treated mainspring housing for use with high-velocity cartridges; heavier barrel; push-button magazine release on top side of frame. Introduced in 1932; dropped 1948.

    Exc.: $895   **VGood:** $695   **Good:** $495

Colt Woodsman (Second Issue) Sport Model

Same specs as the Second Issue Woodsman except 4½-inch barrel; 9-inch overall length; plastic grips. Introduced 1947; dropped 1955.

    Exc.: $895   **VGood:** $695   **Good:** $495

Colt Woodsman (Second Issue) Match Target 4½-inch

Same specs as Second Issue Woodsman except 4½-inch heavy barrel. Introduced 1947; dropped 1955.

    Exc.: $1295   **VGood:** $995   **Good:** $695

Colt Woodsman (Second Issue) Match Target 6-inch

Same specs as Second Issue Woodsman except flat-sided 6-inch heavy barrel; 10½-inch overall length; 22 LR, standard- or high-velocity; checkered walnut or plastic grips; click-adjustable rear sight, ramp front; blued. Introduced 1947; dropped 1955.

    Exc.: $1095   **VGood:** $895   **Good:** $600

Courtesy Dixie Gunworks

COLT CHALLENGER

Semi-automatic; 22LR; 6- or 4½-inch barrel and fixed sights. Colt's first economy model. Serial numbers begin with 1-C. Total production approximately 77,000. Introduced 1950, replaced by the Huntsman in the latter 1950s.

    Exc.: $550   **VGood:** $325   **Good:** $250

Did You Know?

The Challenger has no magazine safety, automatic slide stop, adjustable sights, push button magazine release, lanyard loop or grip adapters.

Paul Goodwin photo

COLT WOODSMAN (Third Issue)

Semi-automatic; 22 LR; 10-shot; 6½-inch barrel; longer grip; larger thumb safety; slide stop magazine disconnector; thumbrest; plastic or walnut grips; magazine catch on bottom of grip; click-adjustable rear sight, ramp front. Introduced 1955; dropped 1977.

    Exc.: $750   **VGood:** $650   **Good:** $450

Colt Woodsman (Third Issue) Sport Model

Same specs as Third Issue Woodsman except 4½-inch barrel. Introduced 1955; dropped 1977.

    Exc.: $750   **VGood:** $650   **Good:** $450

Colt Woodsman (Third Issue) Match Target 4½-inch

Same specs as Third Issue Woodsman except 4½-inch heavy barrel. Introduced 1955; dropped 1977.

    Perf.: $600   **Exc.:** $550   **VGood:** $500

Colt Woodsman (Third Issue) Match Target 6-inch

Same specs as Third Issue Woodsman except 6-inch heavy barrel. Introduced 1955; dropped 1977.

    Perf.: $950   **Exc.:** $850   **VGood:** $600

Paul Goodwin photo

COLT ACE

Semi-automatic; 22 LR only, standard or high velocity; 4¾-inch barrel; 8¼-inch overall length; no floating chamber; adjustable rear, fixed front sight; target barrel; hand-honed action. Built on same frame as Government Model 45 automatic. Introduced 1931; dropped 1947.

Exc.: $2500   **VGood:** $1800   **Good:** $1100

Paul Goodwin photo

COLT ACE SERVICE MODEL

Semi-automatic; 22 LR, standard or high velocity; 10-shot magazine; identical to Colt National Match. Specially designed chamber increases recoil four-fold to approximate that of 45 auto. Introduced 1937; dropped 1945; reintroduced 1978; dropped 1982.

Old model
Exc.: $3000   **VGood:** $2250   **Good:** $1500

New model
Perf.: $600   **Exc.:** $500   **VGood:** $450

Paul Goodwin photo

COLT HUNTSMAN, TARGETSMAN

Semi-automatic; 22 LR; 4½-inch, 6-inch barrel; 9-inch overall length; checkered plastic grips; no hold-open device; fixed sights (Huntsman), adjustable sights and 6-inch barrel only (Targetsman). Introduced 1955; dropped 1977.

Huntsman
Exc.: $595   **VGood:** $495   **Good:** $350

Targetsman
Exc.: $650   **VGood:** $495   **Good:** $350

Did You Know?

The only difference between these two models is the Targetsman has an adjustable rear sight, a thumbrest on the left grip panel, and was only available with a 6-inch barrel.

Paul Goodwin photo

COLT GOLD CUP NATIONAL MATCH MKIII

Semi-automatic; 45 ACP, 38 Spl.; 5-inch match barrel; 8½-inch overall length; weighs 37 oz.; Patridge front sight, Colt Elliason adjustable rear; arched or flat housing; wide, grooved trigger with adjustable stop; ribbed top slide; hand-fitted with improved ejection port. Introduced 1959; dropped 1970.

45 ACP
Exc.: $1000   **VGood:** $800   **Good:** $650

38 Spl.
Exc.: $1100   **VGood:** $850   **Good:** $700

Paul Goodwin photo

COLT GOLD CUP NATIONAL MATCH MKIV SERIES 70

Semi-automatic; 45 ACP; 7-shot magazine; 5-inch barrel; 8⅜-inch overall length; weighs 38½ oz.; undercut front sight, Colt Elliason adjustable rear; match-grade barrel, bushing; long, wide grooved trigger; flat grip housing; hand-fitted slide; checkered walnut grips; blued finish. Introduced 1970; dropped 1983.

Exc.: $1150 **VGood:** $895 **Good:** $700

Paul Goodwin photo

COLT COMBAT COMMANDER (Pre-1970)

Semi-automatic; single action; 45 ACP, 38 Super, 9mm Para.; 7-shot (45 ACP), 9-shot (38 Super, 9mm); 4¼-inch barrel; 7⅞-inch overall length; weighs 35 oz.; fixed sights; thumb grip safeties; steel or alloy frame; grooved trigger; walnut grips; blue or satin nickel finish. Introduced 1950; dropped 1976.

45 ACP, 38 Super
Exc.: $800   **VGood:** $600   **Good:** $400

9mm
Exc.: $600   **VGood:** $450   **Good:** $300

Paul Goodwin photo

COLT COMBAT COMMANDER MKIV SERIES 70

Semi-automatic; single action; 45 ACP, 38 Super, 9mm Para.; 7-shot (45 ACP), 9-shot (38 Super, 9mm); 4¼-inch barrel; 7⅞-inch overall length; weighs 36 oz.; fixed blade front sight; square notch rear; all steel frame; grooved trigger; lanyard-style hammer; checkered walnut grips; blue or nickel finish. Introduced in 1970; dropped 1983.

Perf.: $750   **Exc.:** $600   **VGood:** $400

Nickel finish
Perf.: $800   **Exc.:** $650   **VGood:** $450

Paul Goodwin photo

COLT COMBAT COMMANDER LIGHTWEIGHT MKIV SERIES 70

Same specs as Combat Commander MKIV Series 70 except 45 ACP; weighs 27 oz.; aluminum alloy frame; Introduced 1970; dropped 1983.

Perf.: $750 **Exc.:** $650 **VGood:** $500

Paul Goodwin photo

COLT COMBAT GOVERNMENT MKIV SERIES 70

Semi-automatic; single action; 45 ACP; 8-shot magazine; 5-inch barrel; 8⅜-inch overall length; weighs 40 oz. Similar to Government Model except higher undercut front sight, white outlined rear; flat mainspring housing; longer trigger; beveled magazine well; angled ejection port; Colt/Pachmayr wrap-around grips; internal firing pin safety. Introduced 1973; dropped 1983.

Perf.: $650   **Exc.:** $550   **VGood:** $450

Courtesy Dixie Gunworks

COLT MODEL 1908 POCKET HAMMERLESS
(First Issue)

Semi-automatic; 380 ACP; 7-shot magazine; 3¾-inch barrel; 7-inch overall length; fixed sights; hammerless; slidelock; grip safety; hard rubber stocks; blued finish. Same general design, specs as Model 1903 Pocket Hammerless. Manufactured from 1908 to 1911.

Exc.: $1000 **VGood:** $800 **Good:** $650

COLT MODEL 1908 POCKET HAMMERLESS
(Second Issue)

Same specs as First Issue sans barrel bushing. Manufactured from 1911 to 1926.

Exc.: $550 **VGood:** $450 **Good:** $375

COLT MODEL 1908 POCKET HAMMERLESS
(Third Issue)

Same specs as Second Issue except safety disconnector installed on guns with serial numbers above 92,894. Introduced 1926; dropped 1945.

Exc.: $550 **VGood:** $450 **Good:** $350

U.S. Property marked
Exc.: $1500 **VGood:** $1250 **Good:** $1000

Paul Goodwin photo

COLT MODEL 1911 COMMERCIAL

Semi-automatic; also known as Government Model; 45 ACP; 7-shot magazine; 5-inch barrel; weighs 39 oz.; checkered walnut grips; fixed sights; blued finish; commercial variations with letter "C" preceding serial number. Introduced 1912; dropped 1923 to be replaced by Model 1911A1. Collector value.

*Early production High Polish Blue
(through s/n 4500)*
Exc.: $12,000   **VGood:** $10,000   **Good:** $7500

Standard model
Exc.: $4500   **VGood:** $3000   **Good:** $1750

Colt Model 1911 British 455

Same specs as standard model but carries "Calibre 455" on right side of slide and may have broad arrow British ordnance stamp; made 1915 to 1916; 11,000 manufactured. Collector value.

Exc.: $3500   **VGood:** $2750   **Good:** $2100

Paul Goodwin photo

COLT MODEL 1911 MILITARY

Same specs as the civilian version except serial numbers not preceded by the letter C; produced from 1912 to 1924; bright blue finish, early production; duller blue during war. Parkerized finish indicates post-war reworking and commands lesser value than original blue finish. Navy issue marked "Model of 1911 U.S. Navy" on slide.

Standard
Exc.: $2000   **VGood:** $1400   **Good:** $850

U.S. Navy marked
Exc.: $6000   **VGood:** $4800   **Good:** $3600

Remington-UMC (21,676)
Exc.: $2200   **VGood:** $1700   **Good:** $950

Springfield Armory (25,767)
Exc.: $2500   **VGood:** $2000   **Good:** $950

Paul Goodwin photo

COLT MODEL 1911A1

Semi-automatic; single action; 45 ACP, 7-shot magazine; 5-inch barrel; 8½-inch overall length; weighs 38 oz.; checkered walnut (early production) or brown composition (military version) grips; ramped blade front sight, fixed high-profile square notch rear; Parkerized finish. Same specs as Model 1911 except longer grip safety spur; arched mainspring housing; finger relief cuts in frame behind trigger; plastic grips. During WWII other firms produced the 1911A1 under Colt license, including Remington-Rand, Ithaca Gun Co., and Union Switch & Signal Co. These government models bear imprint of licensee on slide. In 1970, this model was redesigned and redesignated as Government Model MKIV Series 70; approximately 850 1911A1 guns were equipped with split-collet barrel bushing and BB prefix serial number which adds to the value. Modern version (marked "Colt M1911A1TM") continues serial number range used on original GI 1911A1 guns and comes with one magazine and molded carrying case. Introduced 1923; still produced.

Commercial model (C s/n)
Exc.: $1250   **VGood:** $1000   **Good:** $850

BB s/n prefix
Exc.: $950   **VGood:** $800   **Good:** $600

COLT MODEL 1911A1 *(cont.)*

Military model
Exc.: $950   **VGood:** $650   **Good:** $500

Singer Mfg. Co. (500)
Exc.: $24,000   **VGood:** $18,500   **Good:** $15,000

Union Switch & Signal (55,000)
Exc.: $2650   **VGood:** $2250   **Good:** $1750

Remington-Rand (1,000,000)
Exc.: $1200   **VGood:** $975   **Good:** $775

Ithaca Gun Co. (370,000)
Exc.: $1250   **VGood:** $1050   **Good:** $850

45/22 conversion unit
Exc.: $650   **VGood:** $550   **Good:** $400

22/45 conversion unit
Exc.: $1500   **VGood:** $1000   **Good:** $800

Colt Government Model MKIV Series 70

Semi-automatic; single action; 45 ACP, 38 Super, 9mm Para.; 7-shot magazine; 5-inch barrel; 8⅜-inch overall length; weighs 40 oz.; ramp front sight, fixed square notch rear; grip, thumb safeties; grooved trigger; accurizor barrel, bushing; blue or nickel (45 only) finish. Redesigned, redesignated Colt Model 1911A1. Introduced 1970; dropped 1983.

Perf.: $925   **Exc.:** $700   **VGood:** $525

Nickel finish
Perf.: $1000   **Exc.:** $750   **VGood:** $550

Paul Goodwin photo

COLT NATIONAL MATCH

Semi-automatic; 45 ACP; 7-shot; 5-inch barrel; 8½-inch overall length; weighs 37 oz.; adjustable rear, ramp front target sight; match-grade barrel; hand-honed action. Also available with fixed sights. Introduced 1933; dropped 1941.

Fixed sights

Exc.: $2750   **VGood:** $2000   **Good:** $1600

Target sights

Exc.: $3250   **VGood:** $2500   **Good:** $1850

Paul Goodwin photo

COLT SUPER 38

Semi-automatic; double action; 38 Colt Super; 9-shot magazine; fixed sights standard, adjustable rear sights available. Same frame as 1911 commercial until 1970. Introduced in 1929. In 1937, the design of the firing pin, safety, hammer, etc. were changed and the model renamed the New Style Super 38. Still in production as Government Model Mark IV/Series 80.

Exc.: $750　　　　**VGood:** $600　　　　**Good:** $500

Pre-WWI

Exc.: $2500　　　　**VGood:** $2000　　　　**Good:** $1500

Paul Goodwin photo

COLT SUPER 38 NATIONAL MATCH

Same specs as Colt Super 38 except hand-honed action; adjustable target sights; match-grade barrel. Manufactured from 1935 to 1941.

Exc.: $4500   **VGood:** $3500   **Good:** $2500

COLT REVOLVERS

Paul Goodwin photo

COLT 357 MAGNUM

Revolver; double action; 357 Mag.; 6-shot swing-out cylinder; 4-inch, 6-inch barrel; 9¼-inch overall length (4-inch barrel); available as service revolver or in target version; latter with wide hammer spur, target grips; checkered walnut grips; Accro rear sight, ramp front; blued finish. Introduced 1953; dropped 1961.

Perf.: $525   **Exc.:** $450   **VGood:** $375

Target Model
Perf.: $600   **Exc.:** $525   **VGood:** $450

Paul Goodwin photo

COLT AGENT (First Issue)

Revolver; double action; 38 Spl.; 6-shot swing-out cylinder; 2-inch barrel; 6¾-inch overall length; weighs 14 oz.; minor variation of Colt Cobra with shorter stub grip for maximum concealment; Colt alloy frame, sideplate; steel cylinder, barrel; no housing around ejector rod; square butt; blued finish. Introduced 1955; dropped 1972.

   Perf.: $300   **Exc.:** $250   **VGood:** $200

Colt Agent (Second Issue)

Same specs as Agent First Issue except 6⅝-inch overall length; weighs 16 oz.; ramp front sight, square notch rear; checkered walnut grips; grip design extends just below bottom of frame. Introduced 1973; dropped 1981.

   Perf.: $250   **Exc.:** $200   **VGood:** $175

Colt Agent (Third Issue)

Same specs as Agent First Issue except shrouded ejector rod; alloy frame; Parkerized-type finish. Introduced 1982; dropped 1986.

   Perf.: $225   **Exc.:** $175   **VGood:** $150

Paul Goodwin photo

COLT ANACONDA

Revolver; double action; 44 Rem. Mag., 45 LC; 6-shot cylinder; 4-inch, 6-inch, 8-inch barrel; 11⅝-inch overall length; weighs 53 oz.; red insert front sight, white-outline adjustable rear; finger-grooved black neoprene combat grips; stainless steel construction; ventilated barrel rib; offset bolt notches in cylinder; full-length ejector rod housing; wide spur hammer. Introduced 1990; no longer produced.

New: $850   **Perf.:** $475   **Exc.:** $400

Paul Goodwin photo

COLT ARMY SPECIAL

Revolver; double action; 32-20, 38 Spl., 41 Colt; 6-shot cylinder; 4-inch, 4½-inch, 5-inch, 6-inch barrels; 9¼-inch overall length (4-inch barrel); 41-caliber frame; hard rubber grips; fixed sights; blued or nickel finish. Not safe for modern 38 Special high-velocity loads in guns chambered for that caliber. Introduced 1908; dropped 1927.

Exc.: $750 **VGood:** $675 **Good:** $500

Did You Know?

James Bond's choice of weapon in the movie "Moonraker" was a long-barreled Colt Army Special.

Paul Goodwin photo

COLT BANKER'S SPECIAL

Revolver; double action; 22 LR (with countersunk chambers after 1932), 38 New Police, 38 S&W; 6-shot swing-out cylinder; 2-inch barrel; 6½-inch overall length; essentially the same as pre-1972 Detective Special, but with shorter cylinder of Police Positive rather than that of Police Positive Special; a few produced with Fitzgerald cutaway trigger guard; checkered hammer spur, trigger; blued or nickel finish. Low production run on 22 gives it collector value. Introduced 1926; dropped 1940.

22 blue finish
Exc.: $1750   **VGood:** $1250   **Good:** $800

22 nickel finish
Exc.: $2250   **VGood:** $1600   **Good:** $1000

38 blue finish
Exc.: $850   **VGood:** $650   **Good:** $400

38 nickel finish
Exc.: $1200   **VGood:** $800   **Good:** $500

Paul Goodwin photo

COLT BUNTLINE SPECIAL

Revolver; single action; 45 Colt; 12-inch barrel; case-hardened frame; hard rubber or walnut grips; designed after guns made as presentation pieces for author Ned Buntline. Introduced 1957; dropped 1992.

2nd Generation (1957-1975)
Perf.: $1695   **Exc.:** $1275   **VGood:** $1000

3rd Generation (1976-1992)
Perf.: $1250   **Exc.:** $850   **VGood:** $700

Paul Goodwin photo

COLT CAMP PERRY MODEL (First Issue)

Single shot; 22 LR, with countersunk chamber for high-velocity ammo after 1930; 10-inch barrel; 13¾-inch overall length; built on frame of Colt Officers Model; checkered walnut grips; hand-finished action; adjustable target sights; trigger, backstrap, hammer spur checkered; blued finish, with top, back of frame stippled to reduce glare. Chamber, barrel are single unit, pivoting to side for loading and extraction. Introduced 1926; dropped 1934.

Exc.: $2000   **VGood:** $1600   **Good:** $1000

Colt Camp Perry Model (Second Issue)

Same specs as First Issue except 8-inch barrel; 12-inch overall length; shorter hammer fall. Only 440 produced. Collector value. Introduced 1934; dropped 1941.

Perf.: $3000   **Exc.:** $2000   **VGood:** $1500

Paul Goodwin photo

COLT COBRA (First Issue)

Revolver; double action; 22 LR, 32 New Police, 38 New Police, 38 Spl.; 6-shot swing-out cylinder; 2-inch, 3-inch, 4-inch, 5-inch barrels; 3-inch, 4-inch, 5-inch barrel styles special order; based on pre-1972 Detective Special, except frame, sideplate of high-tensile aluminum alloy; Coltwood plastic grips on later guns, checkered wood on early issues; square butt, early issue, replaced by round butt; optional hammer shroud; blue finish, matted on top, rear of frame; shrouded ejector rod (later issue). Introduced 1951; dropped 1972.

Perf.: $445   **Exc.:** $325   **VGood:** $250

Nickel finish
Perf.: $475   **Exc.:** $355   **VGood:** $295

22 LR
Perf.: $525   **Exc.:** $395   **VGood:** $300

Colt Cobra (Second Issue)

Same specs as Cobra First Issue except integral protective shroud enclosing ejector rod. Introduced 1973; dropped 1981.

Perf.: $400   **Exc.:** $350   **VGood:** $295

Paul Goodwin photo

COLT COMMANDO

Revolver; double action; 38 Spl.; 6-shot cylinder; 2-inch, 4-inch, 6-inch barrels; plastic grips; sand-blasted blue finish. Government contract issue made to military specs; a downgraded version of the Colt Official Police. Introduced 1942; dropped 1945.

Exc.: $450   **VGood:** $325   **Good:** $250

Did You Know?

The Colt Commando was
manufactured for use in
World War II. General Eisenhower
is reported to have had
one of these guns.

Paul Goodwin photo

COLT DETECTIVE SPECIAL (FIRST ISSUE)

Revolver; double action; 38 Spl.; 6-shot swing-out cylinder; 2-inch, 3-inch barrels; 6¾-inch overall length; rounded butt introduced in 1934; blue or nickel finish. Introduced 1927; dropped 1936.

> **Exc.:** $850   **VGood:** $725   **Good:** $650
>
> *Nickel finish*
> **Exc.:** $900   **VGood:** $800   **Good:** $725

Colt Detective Special (Second Issue)

Same specs as First Issue except 32 New Police, 38 New Police; heavier barrel; integral protective shroud enclosing ejector rod; frame, sideplate, cylinder, barrel, internal parts of high-tensile alloy steel; plastic or walnut Bulldog-type grips; fixed rear sight; notch milled in topstrap, serrated ramp front; checkered hammer spur; blue or nickel finish. Introduced 1947; dropped 1972.

> **Perf.:** $450   **Exc.:** $350   **VGood:** $275
>
> *Nickel finish*
> **Perf.:** $475   **Exc.:** $375   **VGood:** $300

Colt Detective Special (Third Issue)

Same specs as Second Issue except 38 Spl.; shrouded ejector rod; wrap-around walnut grips. Introduced 1973; dropped 1986.

> **Perf.:** $475   **Exc.:** $325   **VGood:** $275

Paul Goodwin photo

COLT DIAMONDBACK

Revolver; double action; 38 Spl., 22 LR; 6-shot swing-out cylinder; 2½-inch, 4-inch (22 LR), 6-inch barrel; vent-rib barrel; scaled-down version of Python; target-type adjustable rear sight, ramp front; full checkered walnut grips; integral rounded rib beneath barrel shrouds, ejector rod; broad checkered hammer spur. Introduced 1966; dropped 1986.

Perf.: $650   **Exc.:** $550   **VGood:** $475

Nickel finish
Perf.: $700   **Exc.:** $650   **VGood:** $550

22 LR
Perf.: $700   **Exc.:** $650   **VGood:** $550

Paul Goodwin photo

COLT FRONTIER SCOUT

Revolver; single action; 22 LR, 22 Long, 22 Short; interchangeable cylinder for 22 WMR; 4½-inch barrel; 9¹⁵⁄₁₆-inch overall length; originally introduced with alloy frame; steel frame, blue finish introduced in 1959; fixed sights; plastic or wooden grips. Introduced 1958; dropped 1971.

Alloy frame
Perf.: $600   **Exc.:** $425   **VGood:** $325

Blue finish, plastic grips
Perf.: $600   **Exc.:** $400   **VGood:** $300

Nickel finish, wood grips
Perf.: $650   **Exc.:** $475   **VGood:** $350

With 22 WMR cylinder
Perf.: $650   **Exc.:** $475   **VGood:** $375

Colt Frontier Scout Buntline

Same specs as Frontier Scout except 9½-inch barrel. Introduced 1959; dropped 1971.

Perf.: $500   **Exc.:** $425   **VGood:** $325

Paul Goodwin photo

COLT LAWMAN MKIII

Revolver; double action; 357 Mag.; also chambers 38 Spl.; 2-inch, 4-inch barrels; 9⅜-inch overall length (4-inch barrel); choice of square, round butt walnut grips; fixed sights; blued, nickel finish. Introduced 1969; dropped 1983.

> **Perf.:** $375   **Exc.:** $275   **VGood:** $225
>
> *Nickel finish*
> **Perf.:** $395   **Exc.:** $295   **VGood:** $250

Colt Lawman MKV

Same specs as Lawman MKIII except redesigned lockwork to reduce double-action trigger pull; faster lock time; redesigned grips; shrouded ejector rod (2-inch barrel); fixed sights; solid rib. Introduced 1984; dropped 1985.

> **Perf.:** $375   **Exc.:** $275   **VGood:** $225
>
> *Nickel finish*
> **Perf.:** $395   **Exc.:** $295   **VGood:** $250

Paul Goodwin photo

COLT MODEL 1917 ARMY

Revolver; double action; 6-shot swing-out cylinder; 45 Auto Rim cartridge can be fired in conventional manner; based upon New Service revolver to fire 45 ACP cartridge with steel half-moon clips; $10^{13}/_{16}$-inch overall length; 5½-inch barrel; smooth walnut grips; fixed sights; dull finish. Should be checked for damage by corrosive primers before purchase. Introduced 1917; dropped 1925.

Exc.: $1375   **VGood:** $1075   **Good:** $895

Paul Goodwin photo

COLT NEW FRONTIER

Revolver; flat-top target version of Colt Single Action Army first introduced in 1962 during 2nd Generation production and continued until 1974. Serial numbers began at 3000NF and ended in 1974 with 7288NF. Calibers offered during 2nd Generation were 45 Colt, 44 Spl., 357 Mag., and 38 Spl. Standard barrel lengths 4¾-inch, 5½-inch, 7½-inch; a total of seventy-two 45 Colt Buntline New Frontiers manufactured with 12-inch barrels. Finish was Colt's royal blue with color case-hardened frame. Two-piece walnut grips were standard. Manufacture of New Frontiers resumed in 1978 during 3rd Generation production and continued until 1985. Serial numbers began again at 01001NF and ran to approximately 17000NF by 1985. During 3rd Generation production, calibers offered were 45 Colt, 44 Spl., and 357 Mag., with 44-40 being added in 1981. Finishes were Colt's royal blue with color case-hardened frame, with fully nickel-plated, and fully-blued being rarely-found options. Barrel lengths were the standard 4-¾-inch, 5½-inch, and 7½-inch.

2nd Generation
Perf.: $1000   **Exc.:** $750   **VGood:** $600

3rd Generation
Perf.: $850   **Exc.:** $650   **VGood:** $500

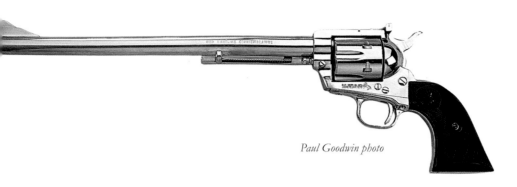

Paul Goodwin photo

COLT NEW FRONTIER BUNTLINE SPECIAL

Same specs as New Frontier except 45 Colt; 12-inch barrel; flat-top frame; adjustable rear sight.

2nd Generation
Perf.: $2500   **Exc.:** $1850   **VGood:** $1250

3rd Generation
Perf.: $2000   **Exc.:** $1500   **VGood:** $1000

Did You Know?

This model is rare, as Colt only manufactured 72 during 1962-1967.

Paul Goodwin photo

COLT NEW FRONTIER 22

Revolver; single action; 6-shot cylinder; furnished with dual cylinders for 22 LR, 22 WMR; 4⅜-inch, 6-inch, 7½-inch barrels; 11½-inch overall length (6-inch barrel); scaled-down version of New Frontier 45; target-type fully-adjustable rear sight, ramp front; checkered black plastic grips; flat topstrap; color case-hardened frame, rest blued. Introduced 1973; dropped 1975; reintroduced 1981; dropped 1982.

    Perf.: $400   **Exc.:** $350   **VGood:** $250

    7½-inch barrel

    Perf.: $375   **Exc.:** $350   **VGood:** $250

Paul Goodwin photo

COLT NEW SERVICE

Revolver; double action; 38 Spl., 357 Mag., 38-40, 38-44, 44 Russian, 44 Spl., 44-40, 45 Colt, 45 ACP, 450 Eley, 455 Eley, 476 Eley; 2-inch, 3½-inch 4-inch, 4½-inch, 5-inch, 5½-inch, 6-inch, 7½-inch barrels; 6-shot swing-out cylinder; large frame. Special run in 45 ACP. During WWI was designated as Model 1917 Revolver under government contract. Fixed open notch rear sight milled in topstrap, fixed front; checkered hard rubber grips on commercial New Service; lanyard loop on most variations; blued, nickel finish. Introduced 1897; dropped 1944.

Commercial model
Exc.: $1975   **VGood:** $1650   **Good:** $1375

Military model
Exc.: $1750   **VGood:** $1275   **Good:** $1125

357 Mag.
Exc.: $1200   **VGood:** $1000   **Good:** $875

Courtesy Dixie Gunworks

COLT NEW SERVICE SHOOTING MASTER

Same specs as New Service except 38 Spl., 357 Mag., 44 Spl., 45 ACP/Auto Rim, 45 Colt; 6-inch barrel; 11¼-inch overall length; deluxe target version; checkered walnut grips, rounded butt; windage-adjustable rear sight, elevation-adjustable front; blued. Introduced 1932; dropped 1941.

38 Special
Exc.: $1350   **VGood:** $1025   **Good:** $900

44 Spl., 45 ACP, 45 Colt
Exc.: $3850   **VGood:** $3425   **Good:** $3050

Colt New Service Target

Same specs as standard New Service model except windage-adjustable rear sight, elevation-adjustable front; 44 Spl., 44 Russian, 45 Colt, 45 ACP, 450 Eley, 455 Eley, 476 Eley; 5-inch, 6-inch, 7½-inch barrels; flat topstrap; finished action; blued finish; hand-checkered walnut grips. Introduced 1900; dropped 1940.

Exc.: $2850   **VGood:** $2575   **Good:** $2100

Paul Goodwin photo

COLT OFFICER'S MODEL TARGET
(First, Second, Third Issues)

Revolver; double action; 38 Spl. (First Issue); 32 Colt, 38 Spl. (Second Issue); 22 LR (Third Issue); 6-shot cylinder; 6-inch barrel (38 Spl.); 4-inch, 4½-inch, 5-inch, 6-inch, 7½-inch barrels (32 Colt, 38 Spl., 22 LR); hand-finished action; adjustable rear target, blade front sight; blued finish. First Issue manufactured 1904-1908; Second Issue, 1908-1926; Third Issue, 1927-1949.

First Issue
Exc.: $1500   **VGood:** $1250   **Good:** $950

Second Issue
Exc.: $1150   **VGood:** $1000   **Good:** $850

Third Issue
Exc.: $825   **VGood:** $750   **Good:** $650

Paul Goodwin photo

COLT OFFICER'S MODEL MATCH

Same specs as Officer's Model Special, which it replaced, except checkered walnut target grips; tapered heavy barrel; wide hammer spur. Introduced 1953; dropped 1970.

Perf.: $425   **Exc.:** $375   **VGood:** $300

Paul Goodwin photo

COLT OFFICER'S MODEL SPECIAL

Same specs as Second Issue Officer's Model Target except heavier barrel; ramp front, Coltmaster adjustable rear sight; redesigned hammer; checkered plastic stocks; 6-inch barrel; 22 LR, 38 Spl.; blued finish. Introduced 1949; dropped 1955.

Exc.: $550   **VGood:** $425   **Good:** $375

Paul Goodwin photo

COLT OFFICIAL POLICE

Revolver; double action; 22 LR, 32-20, 38 Spl., 41 Long Colt; 6-shot cylinder; 2-inch, 6-inch heavy barrels (38 Spl. only); 4-inch, 6-inch barrels (22 LR only); 4-inch, 5-inch, 6-inch (other calibers); checkered walnut grips, plastic grips on post-WWII models. Version made to military specs in WWII was called Commando model, had sand-blasted blue finish. Introduced 1927 as a replacement for Army Special; dropped 1970. Collector value.

Perf.: $525   **Exc.:** $425   **VGood:** $350

Military model
Perf.: $550   **Exc.:** $460   **VGood:** $375

Colt Official Police MkIII

Revolver; double action; 38 Spl.; 4-inch, 5-inch, 6-inch barrels; 9⅜-inch overall length; an old name, but a renewed design, incorporating coil mainspring in place of leaf spring; square butt, checkered walnut grips; fixed rear sight notch milled in topstrap, fixed ramp front; grooved front surface on trigger; checkered hammer spur. Introduced 1969; dropped 1975.

Perf.: $325   **Exc.:** $275   **VGood:** $225

Paul Goodwin photo

COLT POCKET POSITIVE

Revolver; double action; 32 Short Colt, 32 Long Colt, 32 Colt New Police (interchangeable with 32 S&W Long, S&W Short cartridges); 6-shot cylinder; 2-inch, 2½-inch, 3½-inch, 4-inch, 5-inch, 6-inch barrels; 7½-inch overall length (3½-inch barrel); rear sight groove milled in topstrap, rounded front sight; positive lock feature; hard rubber grips; blued or nickel finish. Based upon New Pocket Model dropped in 1905. Introduced 1905; dropped 1940.

> **Exc.:** $525   **VGood:** $465   **Good:** $385
>
> *Nickel finish*
> **Exc.:** $625   **VGood:** $550   **Good:** $475

Paul Goodwin photo

COLT POLICE POSITIVE

Revolver; double action; 32 Short Colt, 32 Long Colt, 32 Colt New Police, 38 S&W; 6-shot swing-out cylinder; 2½-inch, 4-inch, 5-inch, 6-inch barrels; 8½-inch overall length (4-inch barrel); fixed sights; checkered walnut, plastic or hard rubber grips; top of frame matted to reduce glare; blue or nickel finish; replaced New Police model. Introduced 1905; dropped 1943. Reintroduced 1995; no longer in production.

Exc.: $450   **VGood:** $395   **Good:** $335

Nickel finish
Exc.: $500   **VGood:** $425   **Good:** $375

Paul Goodwin photo

COLT POLICE POSITIVE SPECIAL
(First, Second, Third Issues)

Same specs as standard Police Positive except lengthened frame to accommodate longer cylinder for 38 Spl., 32-20; also made in 32 and 38 Colt New Police; 4-inch, 5-inch, 6-inch barrels; 8¾-inch overall length (4-inch barrel); blued or nickel. Introduced 1908; dropped 1970. Reintroduced 1995; no longer produced.

Perf.: $495   **Exc.:** $450   **VGood:** $395

Colt Police Positive Target

Same specs as standard Police Positive except 32 Short Colt, 32 Long Colt, 32 New Police, 32 S&W Short, 32 S&W Long, 22 LR. In 1932, cylinder was modified by countersinking chambers for safety with high-velocity 22 ammo; those with non-countersunk chambers should be fired only with standard-velocity 22 LR ammo. Has 6-inch barrel; 10½-inch overall length, windage-adjustable rear sight, elevation-adjustable front; checkered walnut grips; blued; backstrap, hammer spur, trigger checkered. Introduced 1905; dropped 1941.

Exc.: $700   **VGood:** $500   **Good:** $300

Paul Goodwin photo

COLT PYTHON

Revolver; double action; 357 Mag., but will handle 38 Spl.; 6-shot swing-out cylinder; made first appearance in 6-inch barrel later with 2½-inch, 3-inch, 4-inch, 8-inch; checkered walnut grips contoured for support for middle finger of shooting hand; vent-rib barrel; ramp front sight, fully-adjustable rear; full-length ejector rod shroud; wide-spur hammer; grooved trigger; blued, nickel finish; hand-finished action. Introduced 1955; no longer produced.

> **Perf.:** $875   **Exc.:** $775   **VGood:** $675
>
> *Nickel finish*
> **Perf.:** $1150   **Exc.:** $825   **VGood:** $675

Colt Python Stainless

Same specs as standard Python except stainless steel construction; 4-inch, 6-inch barrel lengths only. Introduced 1983; no longer produced.

> **Perf.:** $975   **Exc.:** $800   **VGood:** $650

Paul Goodwin photo

COLT SINGLE ACTION ARMY

Colt Single Action Army also known as Peacemaker, or Frontier Six Shooter (44-40 caliber only). Originally introduced in 1873 and produced continuously until 1941. This production is run known as "1st Generation." The production run resumed in 1956 and stopped again in 1974 is known as "2nd Generation." Production known as "3rd Generation" began in 1976 and is still being manufactured. 1st Generation serial numbers began in 1873 with #1 and ended in 1941 with serial number 357859. The first Generation production included two frame styles: From 1873 until 1892, frames had screw angling in from front of frame to secure cylinder base pin; starting in 1892, and becoming standard by 1896, cylinder pin is secured by spring-loaded transverse catch. These frames are mistakenly called "blackpowder" and "smokeless powder" frames respectively, but it should be noted that Colt did not warranty any SAA revolvers for smokeless powder until 1900 at about serial number 192000. Rarer calibers and barrel lengths bring considerable premium over prices shown. When 2nd Generation production began in 1956, serial numbers started at #0001SA, and continued until approximately #74000SA. 3rd Generation production started in 1976 and serial numbers resumed at #80000SA. When #99999SA was reached in 1978, the SA was made a prefix and numbers started once more at #SA00001. When #SA99999 was reached about 1993, the SA was split and numbers started once more at #S0001A. Standard barrel lengths for all three generations have been 4¾-inch (introduced 1879), 5½-inch (introduced 1875), and 7½-inch (introductory length

COLT SINGLE ACTION ARMY *(cont.)*

offered in 1873). Standard finishes for all three generations have been color case-hardened frame with remainder blued, or fully nickel-plated. Some fully-blued SAAs have been offered by Colt from time to time. For 1st Generation, standard grips were one-piece walnut in early production and two-piece hard rubber in later production. Standard grips in 2nd Generation were hard rubber, and both hard rubber and two-piece walnut in 3rd Generation. Standard sights were groove down revolver's topstrap and blade front. Caliber options for 1st Generation revolvers numbered approximately thirty, ranging from 22 rimfire to 476 Eley. However, the top five in terms of numbers produced were 45 Colt, 44-40, 38-40, 32-20 and 41 Colt. 2nd Generation calibers in order of numbers produced were 45 Colt, 357 Magnum, 38 Special, 44 Spl. 3rd Generation calibers started in 1976 with 45 Colt and 357 Mag. In 1978, 44 Spl. was added, and in 1980 44-40 was included once more. In 1993, 38-40 was made an option again. 2nd Generation Buntline and Sheriff's Models made only in 45 Colt from 1957 until 1974. 3rd Generation Buntline and Sheriff's Models made in 45 Colt, 44-40, and 44 Spl. calibers from 1980 until 1985. So-called "blackpowder frame" model with screw angling in from front of frame to secure cylinder base pin re-introduced in 1984 and offered as custom feature until early 1990s. During period 1984 to 1994, Colt SAAs could be ordered from Colt Custom Shop with almost any combination of features listed above.

1st Generation (s/n up to 357859, common models)
Exc.: $7500   **VGood:** $4500   **Good:** $3000

2nd Generation (s/n #0001SA to #74000SA)
Exc.: $1600   **VGood:** $1200   **Good:** $800

3rd Generation (s/n #80000SA to present)
Perf.: $1200   **Exc.:** $800   **VGood:** $700

COLT SINGLE ACTION

Revolver; single action; 44-40, 45 Colt, 6-shot. Barrel: 4¾-inch, 5½-inch, 7½-inch. Weight: 40 oz. (4¾-inch barrel). Length: 10¼-inch overall (4¾-inch barrel). Stocks: Black Eagle composite. Sights: Blade front, notch rear. Features: Available in full nickel finish with nickel grip medallions, or Royal Blue with color case-hardened frame, gold grip medallions. Reintroduced 1992.

New: $1200   **Perf.:** $1000   **Exc.:** $850

Paul Goodwin photo

COLT TROOPER

Revolver; double action; 22 LR, 38 Spl., 357 Mag.; 6-shot swing-out cylinder; ramp front sight; choice of standard hammer, service grips, wide hammer spur, target grips. Has the same specs as Officer's Match model except 4-inch barrel. Introduced 1953; dropped 1969.

Exc.: $450   **VGood:** $300   **Good:** $275

Target model
Exc.: $475   **VGood:** $325   **Good:** $300

Paul Goodwin photo

COLT TROOPER MKIII

Revolver; double action; 22 LR, 22 WMR, 38 Spl., 357 Mag.; 4-inch, 6-inch, 8-inch barrels; 9½-inch overall length (4-inch barrel); rear sight fully-adjustable, ramp front; shrouded ejector rod; checkered walnut target grips; target hammer; wide target trigger; blued, nickel finish. Introduced 1969; dropped 1983.

Perf.: $525   **Exc.:** $425   **VGood:** $375

Nickel finish

Perf.: $600   **Exc.:** $500   **VGood:** $425

FREEDOM ARMS, INC.

314 Highway 239
PO Box 150
Freedom Wyoming 83120
Phone: *800-252-4867*

In the late 1970s the Freedom Arms company was formed and assumed production of a line of stainless steel mini-revolvers that had been made previously by both Rocky Mountain Arms and North American Arms, and then introduced what would prove to be their flagship product, the single-action 454 Casull revolver.

Demand for the well-made stainless steel single action in the powerful Casull chambering grew to require all the company's resources and, in 1989, Freedom Arms left the mini-revolver business to concentrate on development and production of their well-made single-action revolver models.

Noted for their exceptionally high quality, the Freedom Arms single actions were chambered for some of the most powerful handgun cartridges available, to include the 454 Casull, 475 Linebaugh and 50 AE. Also offered were the "standard" handguns chamberings: 357 Magnum, 41 Magnum, 44 Magnum and 45 Colt.

The 22 rimfire was not neglected and the company introduced a single action specifically designed for the rimfire round, then went on to offer the rimfire chambering in several other models with a choice of match or sport chambers.

Production quantities were never high, and the company was able to offer a variety of options, to include octagon barrels, match sights, and non-standard barrel lengths. The guns were expensive, but the quality supported the price and knowledgeable handgunners dreamed of owning their own Freedom Arms single action.

FREEDOM ARMS MINI REVOLVER

Revolver; single action; 22 LR, 22 WMR; 5-shot; 4-inch (22 WMR), 1-inch, 1¾-inch barrel (22 LR); 4-inch overall length; blade front sight, notched rear; black ebonite grips; stainless steel construction; marketed in presentation case. Introduced 1978; dropped 1990.

Perf.: $210   **Exc.:** $185   **VGood:** $165

HARRINGTON & RICHARDSON

H&R 1871, LLC
100 Kenna Drive
North Haven, Conn. 06473
Phone: *203-239-5621*
Website: *www.marlinfirearms.com*

Today H&R Firearms is owned by the Marlin Firearms Company, and manufactures single-shot shotguns (predominantly) in their Gardner, Massachusetts factory.

The first Harrington & Richardson company was founded in 1871 as Wesson & Harrington and, over the decades, the business occupied as many as four locations, all on Park Avenue in Worcester, Massachusetts.

The old H&R company went out of business in 1986, and the building was demolished. A few years later, in 1991, a new company, H&R 1871, Inc., was formed and resumed production of revolvers, single-shot rifles and shotguns using old H&R designs.

In 2000, H&R 1871, Inc. was sold to Marlin Firearms and remains under their ownership today.

Courtesy Dixie Gunworks

HARRINGTON & RICHARDSON AUTOMATIC EJECTING MODEL

Revolver; double action; 32 S&W Long, 38 S&W; 6-shot cylinder (32), 5-shot (38); 3¼-inch, 4-inch, 5-inch, 6-inch barrel; weighs 16 oz.; hinged-frame; fixed sights; hard rubber or checkered walnut target grips; blued, nickel finish. Introduced 1891; dropped 1941.

Exc.: $160   **VGood:** $150   **Good:** $105

Did You Know?

The top-breaking, shell-ejecting revolver was invented by Gilbert Harrington, one of the two founders of the original company.

Paul Goodwin photo

HARRINGTON & RICHARDSON NO. 199

Revolver; single action; 22 LR; 9-shot cylinder; 6-inch barrel; 11-inch overall length; weighs 30 oz.; hinged frame; adjustable target sights; checkered walnut grips; blued finish. Single action version of the double-action Model 999 Sportsman. Introduced 1933; dropped 1951.

Exc.: $125   **VGood:** $110   **Good:** $85

Paul Goodwin photo

HARRINGTON & RICHARDSON TRAPPER MODEL

Revolver; double action; 22 Short, 22 Long, 22 LR; 7-shot cylinder; 6-inch octagonal barrel; weighs 12¼ oz.; solid frame; gold front sight; checkered walnut stocks; blued finish. Introduced 1924; dropped during WWII.

Exc.: $100   **VGood:** $90   **Good:** $75

Paul Goodwin photo

HARRINGTON & RICHARDSON USRA MODEL

Single shot; 22 LR; 7-inch, 8-inch, 10-inch barrel; weighs 31 oz. (10-inch barrel); hinged frame target pistol; adjustable target sights; adjustable trigger pull; checkered walnut grips; blued finish. Introduced 1928; dropped 1943.

    Exc.: $450   **VGood:** $350   **Good:** $250

Did You Know?

This pistol was adopted
by the U.S. Army Pistol Team
because of its accuracy.

Paul Goodwin photo

HARRINGTON & RICHARDSON 22 SPECIAL

Revolver; double action; 22 Short, 22 Long, 22 LR, 22 WMR; 9-shot cylinder; 6-inch barrel; 11-inch overall length; weighs 23 oz.; heavy hinged-frame; fixed notch rear sight, gold-plated front; checkered walnut grips; blued. Originally introduced as Model 944; later version with recessed cylinder for high-speed ammo was listed as Model 945. Introduced 1925; dropped 1941.

Exc.: $165   **VGood:** $140   **Good:** $120

Courtesy Dixie Gunworks

HARRINGTON & RICHARDSON MODEL 40 HAMMERLESS

Revolver; double action; 22 LR, 32 S&W Short; 7-shot cylinder (22), 5-shot (32); 2-inch, 3-inch, 4-inch, 5-inch, 6-inch barrels; fixed sights; small hinged-frame; hard rubber stocks; blued or nickel finish. Also listed during late production as Model 45. Introduced 1899; dropped 1941.

Exc.: $150   **VGood:** $85   **Good:** $65

Did You Know?

Harrington & Richardson introduced their first double-action gun in 1878.

Courtesy Dixie Gunworks

HARRINGTON & RICHARDSON MODEL 50 HAMMERLESS

Revolver; double action; 32 S&W Long, 38 S&W; 6-shot cylinder (32), 5-shot (38); 3¼-inch, 4-inch, 5-inch, 6-inch barrels; fixed sights; small hinged-frame; hard rubber stocks; blued or nickel finish. Also listed during late production as Model 55. Introduced 1899; dropped 1941.

Exc.: $135   **VGood:** $80   **Good:** $60

Did You Know?

By 1908, three million revolvers exhibiting the Harrington & Richardson trademarks had been made.

HARRINGTON & RICHARDSON MODEL 649

Revolver; double action; two 6-shot cylinders; 22 LR, 22 WMR; 5½-inch, 7½-inch barrel; solid frame; blade front, adjustable rear sight; one-piece walnut grip; blued finish. Introduced in 1976; dropped 1980.

Exc.: $140   **VGood:** $120   **Good:** $110

HARRINGTON & RICHARDSON MODEL 676

Revolver; double action; 22 LR, 22 WMR; two 6-shot cylinders; 4½-inch, 5½-inch, 7½-inch, 12-inch barrel; solid frame; blade front, adjustable rear sight; one-piece walnut grip; color case-hardened frame; blued finish. Introduced 1976; dropped 1985.

Exc.: $140   **VGood:** $120   **Good:** $100

HARRINGTON & RICHARDSON MODEL 686

Revolver; double action; 22 LR, 22 WMR; two 6-shot cylinders; 5½-inch, 7½-inch, 10-inch, 12-inch barrel; ramp and blade front sight, fully-adjustable rear; one-piece walnut grip; color case-hardened frame; blued finish. Introduced 1981; dropped 1985.

Exc.: $185   **VGood:** $160   **Good:** $140

HARRINGTON & RICHARDSON MODEL 949

Revolver; double action; 22 LR, Long, Short; 9-shot cylinder; 5½-inch barrel; solid-frame; side-loading, ejection; adjustable rear sight, blade front; one-piece plain walnut grip; blued, nickel finish. Advertised as Forty-Niner Model. Introduced in 1960; dropped, 1985.

Exc.: $115   **VGood:** $100   **Good:** $85

Harrington & Richardson Model 949 Western

Revolver; double action; 22 LR; 9-shot cylinder; 5½-inch, 7½-inch barrel; weighs 36 oz.; walnut-stained hardwood grips; blade front sight, adjustable rear; color case-hardened frame and backstrap; traditional loading gate and ejector rod. Made in U.S. by Harrington & Richardson. Introduced 1994; no longer produced.

New: $140   **Perf.:** $125   **Exc.:** $110

HARRINGTON & RICHARDSON MODEL 976

Revolver; double action; 22 LR, 38 S&W; 9-shot cylinder (22 LR), 5-shot (38 S&W); 4-inch barrel; hinged frame; fixed front, adjustable rear sight; checkered walnut stocks; blued finish. Introduced 1968; dropped 1981.

Exc.: $110 **VGood:** $90 **Good:** $85

Paul Goodwin photo

HARRINGTON & RICHARDSON MODEL 999

Revolver; double action; 22 Short, 22 Long, 22 LR; 9-shot cylinder; 4-inch, 6-inch top-break barrel; weighs 34 oz.; checkered hardwood grips; elevation-adjustable front sight, windage-adjustable rear; automatic ejection; triggerguard extension; blued finish; optional engraving. Marketed as Sportsman Model. Introduced 1936; dropped 1985.

Exc.: $195   **VGood:** $170   **Good:** $155

Engraved
Exc.: $425   **VGood:** $375   **Good:** $300

Paul Goodwin photo

HARRINGTON & RICHARDSON MODEL 999 SPORTSMAN

Revolver; double action; 22 LR; 9-shot cylinder; 4-inch, 6-inch barrel; 8½-inch overall length; weighs 30 oz.; walnut-finished hardwood grips; elevation-adjustable blade front sight, windage-adjustable rear; top-break loading; automatic shell ejection; polished blue finish. Made in U.S. by Harrington & Richardson. Reintroduced 1992; no longer in production.

Perf.: $275   **Exc.:** $225   **VGood:** $175

HARRINGTON & RICHARDSON MODEL 171

Single shot; trap door action; 45-70; 22-inch barrel; 41-inch overall length; weighs 7 lbs.; open fully-adjustable rear, blade front sight; uncheckered American walnut stock. Replica of Model 1873 Springfield cavalry carbine. Introduced 1972; discontinued 1985.

    Exc.: $325   **VGood:** $275   **Good:** $200

Harrington & Richardson Model 171 Deluxe

Same specs as Model 171 except folding leaf rear sight; engraved breechblock, side lock, hammer. Introduced 1972; discontinued 1985.

    Exc.: $420   **VGood:** $375   **Good:** $275

HARRINGTON & RICHARDSON MODEL 172

Single shot; trapdoor action; 45-70; 22-inch barrel; 41-inch overall length; weighs 7 lbs.; tang-mounted aperture sight; fancy checkered walnut stock; silver-plated hardware. Introduced 1972; discontinued 1977.

Exc.: $695   **VGood:** $595   **Good:** $475

Did You Know?

H&R 1871, LLC is currently the largest manufacturer of single shot shotguns and rifles in the world.

HARRINGTON & RICHARDSON MODEL 173

Single shot; trapdoor action; 45-70; 26-inch barrel; 44-inch overall length; weighs 8 lbs.; Vernier tang rear, blade front sight; engraved breechblock receiver, hammer, barrel band, lock, buttplate; checkered walnut stock; ramrod. Replica of Model 1873 Springfield Officer's Model. Introduced 1972; discontinued 1977.

Exc.: $695   **VGood:** $595   **Good:** $495

HIGH STANDARD MANUFACTURING CO., INC.

5200 Mitchelldale, Ste. E17
Houston, TX 77092
Phone: *800-272-7816*
Website: *www.highstandard.com*

The company was founded in Connecticut in 1926 to supply parts and machine tools to the numerous firearms companies located in the Connecticut River valley. In 1932, the company, headed by Carl Gustav Swebilius, purchased the Hartford Arms and Equipment Company and began making 22-caliber pistols.

High Standard 22-caliber pistols were used to train servicemen in World War II and, by the 1950s, the High Standard 22 pistol was popular on the NRA pistol competition circuit. During this time, the company expanded its offerings, adding derringers, 22 revolvers, 22 rifles and sporting and police shotguns, and began to manufacture private label firearms for the major mass merchants, such as the J.C. Higgins line for Sears.

In the early '60s, the company made some significant design changes. Newly-designed 22 rimfire pistols featured a grip with the same angle as that of the Colt 1911 pistol, and continued to use the handy push-button barrel takedown design and micro-adjustable sights.

In 1968, the company was purchased by the Leisure Group, a growing conglomerate, just as the Gun Control Act of 1968 caused mass merchandisers (nearly 60 percent of High Standard's business) to drastically curtail firearms sales, and the company had to downsize.

By 1975 assets, such as the Hamden plant and the museum, were sold and the company relocated to East Hartford in 1976.

In 1978 a group of investors bought High Standard from the Leisure Group. Things were relatively stable until 1982 when sales of rifles, shotguns and revolvers dwindled. The still-popular derringers and target pistols alone could not carry the load.

In December 1984, the company's assets were auctioned and Gordon Elliott, the national parts distributor for High Standard since the mid-1970s, purchased the 22 target pistols, the Crusader line and the High Standard name and trademarks.

In the spring of 1993, High Standard Manufacturing Company, Inc. of Houston, Texas acquired the company assets and trademarks, as well as the 22 target pistols. The first shipments of Houston-manufactured pistols began in March, 1994 and continue to the present.

Did You Know?

In 1960, Lieutenant Colonel William McMillan won the Gold Medal in the Olympic Rapid Fire competition using a High Standard pistol.

Paul Goodwin photo

HI-STANDARD MODEL H-D

Semi-automatic; 22 LR; 10-shot magazine; 4½-inch, 6¾-inch barrel; 11½-inch overall length (6¾-inch barrel); adjustable target-type sights; deluxe checkered walnut grips with thumb rest. Same as the Model D except visible hammer and no thumb safety. Introduced 1940; dropped 1942. Approximately 6900 produced.

> **Exc.:** $900   **VGood:** $700   **Good:** $550

Hi-Standard Model H-D U.S.A.

Semi-automatic; 22 LR; 10-shot magazine; 4½-inch, 6¾-inch barrels; adjustable target-type sights; medium weight barrel; thumb safety; black or checkered hard rubber grips; high polish blue (early models), Parkerized finish. U.S. military training pistol. Introduced 1943; dropped 1946. Approximately 44,000 produced.

> **Exc.:** $950   **VGood:** $500   **Good:** $400

Hi-Standard H-D U.S.A. Military

Same specs as Model H-D U.S.A. except adjustable sights. Introduced 1946; dropped 1955. Approximately 150,000 produced.

> **Exc.:** $700   **VGood:** $500   **Good:** $350

Paul Goodwin photo

HI-STANDARD SPORT KING (First Model)

Semi-automatic; 22 LR; 10-shot magazine; 4½-inch, 6¾-inch lightweight interchangeable barrels; 11½-inch overall length (6¾-inch barrel); lever takedown; fixed sights; optional adjustable sight; checkered thumb rest plastic grips; blue finish. Introduced 1950; dropped 1953.

Two barrels
Exc.: $600   **VGood:** $500   **Good:** $400

One barrel
Exc.: $400   **VGood:** $300   **Good:** $250

Hi-Standard Sport King (101 Series)

Same specs as First Model except push-button takedown; all-steel frame and slide. Marked "SK-100" or "SK-101" on right side of slide. Introduced 1954; dropped 1984.

Two barrels
Exc.: $600   **VGood:** $500   **Good:** $400

One barrel
Exc.: $400   **VGood:** $300   **Good:** $250

Hi-Standard Sport King Lightweight (101 Series)

Same specs as 101 Series Sport King except forged aluminum alloy frame; weighs 30 oz. (6¾-inch barrel). Marked "Lightweight" on left side of frame. Introduced 1954; dropped 1964.

Two barrels
Exc.: $675   **VGood:** $575   **Good:** $525

One barrel
Exc.: $500   **VGood:** $425   **Good:** $375

Paul Goodwin photo

HI-STANDARD VICTOR (First Model 107 Series)

Semi-automatic; 22 LR only; 10-shot magazine; 4½-inch, 5½-inch barrels; 8¾-inch overall length (4½-inch barrel); 48 oz. (4½-inch barrel), 52 oz. (5½-inch barrel); hammerless; solid steel rib, later guns with aluminum vented rib; interchangeable barrel feature; rib-mounted click-adjustable rear sight, undercut ramp front; checkered walnut grips with thumb rest; blued finish. Marked "The Victor" on left side of barrel. Introduced 1963; dropped 1984.

Solid rib

Exc.: $750   **VGood:** $650   **Good:** $450

Vent rib

Exc.: $800   **VGood:** $700   **Good:** $475

Hi-Standard Victor (ML Series)

Same specs as standard Victor except marked "Victor" above triggerguard. Serial number prefixed with letters "ML."

Exc.: $550   **VGood:** $450   **Good:** $350

Hi-Standard Victor (Seven Number Series)

Same specs as Model 107 except seven-digit serial number appears alone on right side of frame.

Exc.: $525   **VGood:** $325   **Good:** $300

Hi-Standard Victor (SH Series)

Same specs as standard Victor except Allen-screw takedown; small grip thumbrest; rib cut-out for shell ejection. Serial number prefixed with letters "SH."

Exc.: $500   **VGood:** $450   **Good:** $350

Paul Goodwin photo

HI-STANDARD DERRINGER

Derringer; double action; 22 LR, 22 Short, 22 WMR; 2-shot; hammerless; over/under 3½-inch barrels; 5⅛-inch overall length; weighs 11 oz.; plastic grips; fixed sights; standard model has blue, nickel finish. Early derringers marked "Hamden Conn." on barrel; later models marked "E. Hartford" on barrel. Presentation model gold-plated, introduced in 1965; dropped 1966. Presentation model has some collector value. Standard model introduced in 1963; dropped 1984.

Early model, blue finish
Exc.: $250   **VGood:** $185   **Good:** $140

Early model, nickel finish
Exc.: $275   **VGood:** $225   **Good:** $150

Late model, blue finish
Exc.: $250   **VGood:** $185   **Good:** $140

Late model, nickel finish
Exc.: $275   **VGood:** $225   **Good:** $150

Presentation model
Exc.: $400   **VGood:** $350   **Good:** $300

Courtesy Dixie Gunworks

HI-STANDARD SENTINEL

Revolver; double action; 22 Short, 22 LR; 9-shot swing-out cylinder; 3-inch, 4-inch, 6-inch barrels; 9-inch overall length (4-inch barrel); weighs 23 oz.; solid aluminum alloy frame; fixed sights; checkered plastic grips; blued or nickel finish. Introduced 1955; dropped 1974.

Blue finish
Exc.: $145   **VGood:** $125   **Good:** $105

Nickel finish
Exc.: $165   **VGood:** $135   **Good:** $115

Hi-Standard Sentinel Deluxe

Same specs as the standard Sentinel except for movable rear sight; two-piece square-butt checkered walnut grips; wide triggers; 4-inch, 6-inch barrels only. Introduced 1957; dropped 1974.

Blue finish
Exc.: $165   **VGood:** $135   **Good:** $115

Nickel finish
Exc.: $185   **VGood:** $145   **Good:** $125

Hi-Standard Sentinel Imperial

Same specs as standard Sentinel model except blade ramp front sight; two-piece checkered walnut grips; onyx-black or nickel finish. Introduced 1962; dropped 1965.

Blue finish
Exc.: $165   **VGood:** $140   **Good:** $125

Nickel finish
Exc.: $175   **VGood:** $150   **Good:** $125

ITHACA GUNS USA, LLC

420 North Walpole Street
Upper Sandusky, OH 43351
Phone: *419-294-4113*
Website: *www.ithacagunsusa.com*

Ithaca, like most other American gunmakers, has had its ups and downs. Like High Standard, Ithaca was owned by a growing conglomerate in the 1970s, General Recreation, with similar end results. Subsequently, the company's assets changed hands several times and, today, the latest Ithaca is located in the Midwest, having departed New York State, perhaps forever.

Although the company made rifles and shotguns—even a few handguns—during its long life, say the name "Ithaca" today, and most people will think of the Model 37 pump shotgun.

Founded in 1883 in Ithaca, New York, the company built its early reputation by building some nice double-barrel shotguns, in a growing variety of grades and models. Along the way, Ithaca acquired other arms manufacturers, to include Lefever Arms Co., Syracuse Arms Co., and others.

In 1937 the Model 37 pump shotgun was introduced, chambered in 12-gauge. The 16 gauge was added in 1938 and, in 1939, the 20-gauge chambering. The Model 37 was redesignated the Model 87 (in 1987) for a while, but subsequently assumed its original designation. In more recent years (1970s-90s), Ithaca imported Fabarm, Perazzi and SKB shotguns. In 2006, Ithaca's new ownership established their business in the Midwest.

Over two million Model 37s have been manufactured, and today's new ownership promises to keep making the model and servicing parts needs for the earlier guns.

Paul Goodwin photo

ITHACA MODEL 37

Slide action; hammerless; takedown; 12-, 16-, 20-ga.; 4-shot tube magazine; 26-inch, 28-inch, 30-inch barrel; hand-checkered American walnut pistol-grip stock, slide handle, or uncheckered stock, grooved slide handle. Introduced 1937; discontinued 1986.

Checkered stock
Perf.: $250   **Exc.:** $200   **VGood:** $160

Uncheckered stock
Perf.: $240   **Exc.:** $190   **VGood:** $150

Ithaca Model 37 $3000 Grade
Same specs as Model 37 except custom-built; hand-finished parts; hand-checkered pistol-grip stock, slide handle of select figured walnut; gold-inlaid engraving; recoil pad. Was listed as $1000 Grade prior to World War II. Introduced 1937; discontinued 1967.
Exc.: $4000   **VGood:** $3500   **Good:** $2800

Ithaca Model 37D Featherlight
Same specs as Model 37 except 12-, 20-ga.; 5-shot magazine; Ithaca Raybar front sight; checkered American walnut pistol-grip stock, beavertail forend; decorated receiver; crossbolt safety; recoil pad. Introduced 1954; discontinued 1981.
Perf.: $280   **Exc.:** $225   **VGood:** $190

Ithaca Model 37 Deerslayer
Same specs as Model 37 except 20-inch, 26-inch barrel bored for rifled slugs; open rifle-type rear sight, ramp front. Introduced 1969; discontinued 1986.
Perf.: $300   **Exc.:** $240   **VGood:** $195

Ithaca Model 37DV Featherweight
Same specs as Model 37 except 12-, 20-ga.; 5-shot magazine; Ithaca Raybar front sight; vent rib; checkered American walnut pistol-grip stock, beavertail forend; decorated receiver; crossbolt safety; recoil pad. Introduced 1962; discontinued 1981.
Perf.: $325   **Exc.:** $240   **VGood:** $210

Ithaca Model 37S Skeet Grade
Same specs as Model 37 except vent rib; checkered stock, extension slide handle. Introduced 1937; discontinued 1955.
Exc.: $445   **VGood:** $375   **Good:** $335

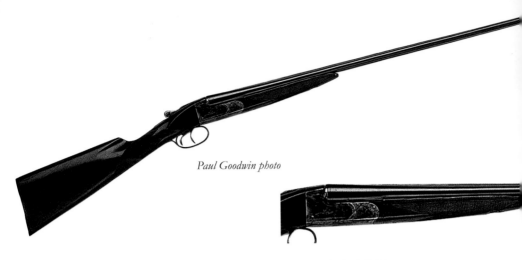

Paul Goodwin photo

NEW ITHACA DOUBLE (NID) FIELD GRADE

Side-by-side; boxlock; hammerless; 10- (3-inch, 3½-inch chambers), 12- (2¾-inch, 3-inch chambers), 16-, 20-ga., .410; 26-inch (12-, 16-, 20-ga., .410), 28-inch (12-, 16-, 20-ga., .410), 30-inch (12-, 16-, 20-ga.), 32-inch (10-ga.), 34-inch (10-ga.) fluid-steel barrels; American walnut pistol-grip stock; extractors (ejectors optional); double triggers (single trigger optional); optional recoil pad, ivory sight. Produced in nine grades. Magnum 10-ga. available in any grade, on special-order only, 1932-1942; total production about 887. Magnum 12-ga. available on special-order only, after 1937; total production about 87. Early NIDs (1926-1936) have snail-ear cocking indicators at the top of the frame. Introduced 1926; discontinued 1948; serial number range: 425000 to 470099.

Exc.: $590   **VGood:** $480   **Good:** $400

New Ithaca Double (NID) Skeet Model Field Grade

Same specs as New Ithaca Double (NID) Field Grade except ivory sight; American walnut pistol-grip stock, beavertail forend; ejectors; recoil pad. Introduced 1935; discontinued 1948.

Exc.: $750   **VGood:** $600   **Good:** $475

New Ithaca Double (NID) No. 2

Same specs as New Ithaca Double (NID) Field Grade.

Exc.: $950   **VGood:** $550   **Good:** $525

New Ithaca Double (NID) No. 3

Same specs as New Ithaca Double (NID) Field Grade; ejectors standard after 1935.

Exc.: $1100   **VGood:** $700   **Good:** $600

New Ithaca Double (NID) No. 4

Same specs as New Ithaca Double (NID) Field Grade except extractors (ejectors optional until 1935, then standard); double triggers (single trigger optional); optional beavertail forend, vent rib, recoil pad, ivory sight.

Exc.: $2250   **VGood:** $1600   **Good:** $1200

Courtesy Dixie Gunworks

ITHACA KNICKERBOCKER ONE-BARREL TRAP GUN NO. 4

Boxlock; hammerless; 12-ga.; 30-inch, 32-inch, 34-inch fluid-steel barrel; vent rib; American walnut straight or pistol-grip stock; recoil pad; ejector; decoration similar to equivalent grades of New Ithaca Double guns; named for its designer, Frank Knickerbocker, it was widely known among shooters as the Knick. Introduced 1922; discontinued 1977, except on special order; serial number range: 400000 to 405739.

Exc.: $1495   **VGood:** $995   **Good:** $750

Ithaca Knickerbocker One-Barrel Trap No. 5

Same specs as Ithaca Knickerbocker One-Barrel Trap Gun No. 4. Introduced 1922; discontinued 1982.

Exc.: $3500   **VGood:** $3000   **Good:** $2500

Ithaca Knickerbocker One-Barrel Trap Victory Grade

Same specs as Ithaca Knickerbocker One-Barrel Trap Gun No. 4 except 32-inch barrel; straight-grip stock. Introduced 1922; discontinued 1937.

Exc.: $795   **VGood:** $600   **Good:** $455

Ithaca Knickerbocker One-Barrel Trap $1000 Grade

Same specs as Ithaca Knickerbocker One-Barrel Trap Gun No. 4. Introduced in 1937 to replace Sousa Special Grade; the name was changed periodically to reflect price increases: $1500 Grade, $2000 Grade, $6500 Grade; after 1980, it was simply Dollar Grade; discontinued 1981.

Perf.: $6000   **Exc.:** $4800   **VGood:** $4000

IVER JOHNSON ARMS, INC.

1840 Baldwin Street, Ste. 7
Rockledge, Florida 32955
Phone: *321-636-3377*

Like its peers, Ithaca and Harrington & Richardson, Iver Johnson traveled a bumpy road subsequent to the company's founding in the latter 1800s. The company was ultimately closed for a period of time, and only recently revived at a new location in Rockledge, Florida. Iver Johnson was a major manufacturer in its day, and probably produced more revolvers than any other armsmaker at the time.

The Iver Johnson revolver designs included both break-top and solid-frame models. The inherent strength, or lack thereof, of the break-top guns restricted their chamberings to the lower-powered cartridges such as 22, 32 and 38. The solid-frame models were relatively unsophisticated designs, but generally nicely finished. Loading and unloading the pistols might require removing the cylinder from the frame and poking out the empties, or flipping open a loading gate and punching out the empties with a barrel-mounted spring-loaded ejector. The break-top models were more efficient at this particular aspect of operation, and popped all the cartridges out simultaneously upon opening.

In more recent years, the company imported Italian single-action revolvers and shotguns.

Paul Goodwin photo

IVER JOHNSON 22 SUPERSHOT SEALED EIGHT
(First Model)

Revolver; double action; 22 LR; 8-shot; 6-inch barrel; 10¾-inch overall length; weighs 24 oz.; large frame; top-break; recessed cylinder chambers; oversize target-type one-piece checkered walnut grips called Hi-Hold by the factory; has "Hammer the Hammer" action; blue finish. Three models: Model 88, fixed sights; Model 833, adjustable sights; Model 834, adjustable sights and adjustable finger rest. Marked 22 SUPERSHOT SEALED EIGHT on left side of barrel. Introduced 1932; dropped 1941.

>   **VGood:** $150   **Good:** $125   **Fair:** $100

Iver Johnson 22 Supershot Sealed Eight (Second Model)

Same specs as First Model except weighs 28 oz.; grip frame modified for ease of manufacture. Two models: Model 88, fixed sights; Model 833, adjustable sights. Marked 22 SUPERSHOT SEALED EIGHT on left side of barrel. Introduced 1946; dropped 1954.

>   **VGood:** $150   **Good:** $125   **Fair:** $100

Iver Johnson 22 Supershot Sealed Eight (Third Model 844)

Same specs as First Model except 4½-inch, 6-inch barrel; 9¼-inch (4¼-inch barrel), 10¾-inch (6-inch barrel) overall length; weighs 27 oz. (4½-inch), 29 oz. (6-inch); unfluted cylinder; flat-sided barrel with full-length rib; recessed cylinder chambers with flash control front rim. Introduced 1955; dropped 1957.

>   **VGood:** $175   **Good:** $150   **Fair:** $125

Paul Goodwin photo

IVER JOHNSON CHAMPION MODEL 36

Single shot; top lever breaking; 12-, 16-, 20-, 24-, 28-ga., .410; 28-inch, 30-inch, 32-inch barrel; Full choke; 45-inch overall length (30-inch barrel); weighs 6-3/4 lbs.; American black walnut stock, forend; rebounding hammer; barrel and lug forged in one; extractor; optional automatic ejector; case-hardened frame, nickel optional; browned barrel; introduced 1909; name changed to Champion Single Barrel Shotgun in 1913; .410, 24-, 28-ga. introduced 1913; 24-ga. discontinued 1928; 16-, 20-, 28-ga., .410 discontinued 1941; 12-ga. discontinued 1957.

Exc.: $125   **VGood:** $100   **Good:** $85

Iver Johnson Champion Model 36 Junior

Same specs as Champion Model 36 except 26-inch barrel; shortened stock. Introduced 1909; dropped 1941.

Exc.: $115   **VGood:** $100   **Good:** $75

Did You Know?

Previously named the "Iver Johnson Arms & Cycle Works," they also produced items such as roller skates, bicycles and handcuffs.

Paul Goodwin photo

IVER JOHNSON HERCULES GRADE HAMMERLESS DOUBLE BARREL

Side-by-side; boxlock; 12-, 16-, 20-ga., .410; 26-inch, 28-inch, 30-inch barrels; 46⅜-inch overall length (30-inch barrels); hand-checkered American black walnut stock with 14-inch pull; .410 has straight stock with 13½-inch pull; stock drop at comb, 1¾-inch; drop at heel, 2¾-inch; plain extractor model with slim forend; automatic ejector model with beavertail forend with D&E fastener; hard rubber buttplate and pistol grip cap; barrels, lugs forged as one then joined together; automatic safety; double triggers. Introduced 1924; discontinued 1941.

Exc.: $650   **VGood:** $550   **Good:** $400

Add 10 percent to above prices for 16 ga.
Add 20 percent for 20 ga.
Add 100 percent for .410 bore
Add 200 percent for 28 ga.

Courtesy Dixie Gunworks

IVER JOHNSON SKEET-ER

Side-by-side; boxlock; 12-, 16-, 20-, 28-ga., .410; 2¾-inch, 3-inch (.410) chamber; optional 2½-inch chamber; 26-inch, 28-inch barrel; 8½ lbs. (12-, 16-, 20-, 28-ga.), 7½ lbs. (.410); Skeet choke, 75 percent at 30 yds. (right barrel), 75 percent at 20 yds. (left); hand-checkered, lacquer-finished select fancy figured American black walnut straight (.410) or pistol-grip stock, large beavertail forend with Deeley & Edge fastener; 14½-inch length; drop at heel 2⅝-inch; hard rubber grip cap; each barrel, lug forged in one, proofed then joined together; automatic extractors or automatic ejectors; automatic or manual safety. Introduced 1927; discontinued 1941.

   Exc.: $1500   **VGood:** $1250   **Good:** $1000

Add 20 percent to above prices for automatic ejectors
Add 50 percent for factory rib vent
Add 20 percent for 20 ga.
Add 40 percent for SST
Add 100 percent for 16 ga., 28 ga. or .410 bore
Add 200 percent for factory engraving (rare)

Paul Goodwin photo

VER JOHNSON TARGET SEALED 8
(First Model)

Revolver; double action; 22 LR; 8-shot; 6-inch (Model 68), 10-inch (Model 78) barrel; 10¾-inch (M68), 14¾-inch (M78) overall length; weighs 24 oz. (M68), 27 oz. (M78); large solid frame; pull pin cylinder release; recessed cylinder chambers; fixed sights, front blade gold-plated; one-piece oversized checkered walnut grips; octagon barrel; does not have "Hammer the Hammer" action. Introduced 1932; dropped 1941.

VGood: $125   **Good:** $100   **Fair:** $75

Courtesy Dixie Gunworks

IVER JOHNSON TARGET SEALED 8
(Second Model)

Same specs as First Model except 4½-inch, 6-inch barrel; 9¼-inch (4½-inch barrel), 10¾-inch (6-inch barrel) overall length; weighs 22½ oz. (4-inch), 24 oz. (6-inch); round barrel. Introduced 1946; dropped 1954.

VGood: $125 **Good:** $100 **Fair:** $75

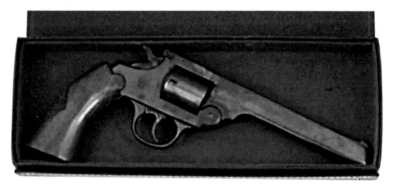

Courtesy Dixie Gunworks

IVER JOHNSON 22 SUPERSHOT SEALED EIGHT
(Third Model 844)

Same specs as First Model except 4½-inch, 6-inch barrel; 9¼-inch (4¼-inch barrel), 10¾-inch (6-inch barrel) overall length; weighs 27 oz. (4½-inch), 29 oz. (6-inch); unfluted cylinder; flat-sided barrel with full-length rib; recessed cylinder chambers with flash control front rim. Introduced 1955; dropped 1957.

VGood: $175 **Good:** $150 **Fair:** $125

Courtesy Dixie Gunworks

IVER JOHNSON MODEL 55 TARGET

Revolver; double action; 22 LR; 8-shot; 4½-inch, 6-inch barrels; 10¾-inch (4¼-inch), 9¼-inch (6-inch) overall length; weighs 24 oz. (4½-inch), 26 oz. (6-inch); large solid frame; pull pin cylinder release with flash control front rim; recessed cylinder chambers; fixed sights; oversize molded one-piece Tenite plastic target-type grips; does not have "Hammer the Hammer" action; matte blue finish. After 1958 cylinder fluted; hard chrome-lined barrel. Introduced 1955; dropped 1960.

VGood: $100 **Good:** $70 **Fair:** $50

Iver Johnson Model 55A

Same specs as Model 55 except incorporation of loading gate; weighs 28½ oz. (4½-inch barrel), 30½ oz. (6-inch barrel). After 1974/1975 this model called the "I J SPORTSMAN." Introduced 1961; dropped 1979.

VGood: $90 **Good:** $70 **Fair:** $50

Iver Johnson Model 55S Cadet

Same specs as Model 55 except 2½-inch barrel; 7-inch overall length; weighs 27 oz.; two-piece small pocket-size grips; fluted cylinder after 1958. Introduced 1955; dropped 1960.

VGood: $110 **Good:** $90 **Fair:** $75

Iver Johnson Model 55S-A Cadet

Same specs as Model 55 except 22 LR, 32 S&W, 38 S&W; 8-shot (22), 5-shot (32, 38); 7-inch overall length; loading gate on right side of frame. After 1974/1975 this model called "I J CADET." Introduced 1961; dropped 1979.

VGood: $110 **Good:** $85 **Fair:** $75

KIMBER

One Lawton Street
Yonkers, NY 10705
Phone: *406-758-2222*

Kimber of Oregon was founded in 1979 by Greg and Jack Warne. The new company produced some 60,000 high-quality rimfire and centerfire rifles before shutting its doors in 1991.

In April of 1993, Greg Warne opened Kimber of America in Clackamas, Oregon. The new company manufactured resumed manufacturing of high-quality rimfire (only) rifles built upon an improved Model 82 action and stock.

In 1995 centerfire rifles were added to the company's offering and, as well, a family of 1911 autoloading pistols chambered for the 45 ACP cartridge. In 1997 manufacturing operations were consolidated in the New York pistol factory and the two manufacturing facilities in Oregon were closed.

Today, Kimber continues to make fine rimfire and centerfire rifles, and 1911-pattern autoloading pistols. Recently, the company added high-quality imported shotguns to their offering.

Although this book focuses on the 1920s through the early 1980s, a U.S.-made Kimber of any vintage is a fine rifle (or pistol), and we should all have one or two in our gun safe.

Paul Goodwin photo

KIMBER MODEL 82

Bolt action; 22 Short, 22 Long, 22 LR, 22 WMR, 22 Hornet; 5-shot magazine (22 Short, 22 Long, 22 LR), 4-shot (22 WMR), 3-shot (22 Hornet); 22-inch, 24-inch barrel; weighs 6½ lbs.; blade front sight on ramp, open adjustable rear; receiver grooved for special Kimber scope mounts; classic-style or Cascade-design select walnut stock; hand-checkered pistol grip, forend; rocker-type silent safety; checkered steel buttplate; steel grip cap; all-steel construction; blued finish. Classic model. Introduced 1980; discontinued 1988.

> **Perf.:** $850 **Exc.:** $695 **VGood:** $595

Kimber Model 82 All-American Match
Same specs as Model 82 except 22 LR; 25-inch target barrel; weighs 9 lbs.; fully-adjustable stock; palm swell, thumb dent pistol grip; step-crowned .9-inch diameter free-floating barrel; forend inletted for weights; adjustable trigger. Introduced 1990; discontinued 1991.

> **Perf.:** $750 **Exc.:** $635 **VGood:** $495

Kimber Model 82, Continental
Same specs as Model 82 except deluxe full-length walnut stock. Introduced 1987; discontinued 1988.

> **Perf.:** $1000 **Exc.:** $900 **VGood:** $695

Kimber Model 82 Government Target
Same specs as Model 82 except 22 LR; 25-inch heavy target barrel; 43½-inch overall length; weighs 10¾ lbs.; oversize target-type Claro walnut stock; single-stage adjustable trigger; designed as U.S. Army trainers. Introduced 1987; discontinued 1991.

> **Perf.:** $600 **Exc.:** $500 **VGood:** $495

Kimber Model 82 SuperAmerica
Same specs as Model 82 except checkered top quality California Claro walnut stock; beaded cheekpiece; ebony forend tip; detachable scope mounts. Introduced 1982; discontinued 1988; reintroduced 1990; discontinued 1991.

> **Perf.:** $1200 **Exc.:** $1100 **VGood:** $1000

Courtesy Kimber

KIMBER MODEL 82C CLASSIC

Bolt action; 22 LR; 4-shot magazine; 21-inch premium air-gauged barrel; 40½-inch overall length; weighs 6½ lbs.; no sights; drilled and tapped for Warne scope mounts optionally available from factory; classic-style stock of Claro walnut; 13½-inch length of pull; hand-checkered; red rubber buttpad; polished steel grip cap; action with aluminum pillar bedding for consistent accuracy; single-set fully-adjustable trigger with 2½-lb. pull. Made in U.S. by Kimber of America, Inc. Reintroduced 1994; no longer produced.

Perf.: $695   **Exc.:** $595   **VGood:** $495

Kimber Model 82C SuperAmerica

Same specs as Model 82C except AAA fancy grade Claro walnut with beaded cheekpiece; ebony forend cap; hand-checkered 22 lpi patterns with wrap-around coverage; black rubber buttpad. Made in U.S. by Kimber of America, Inc. Reintroduced 1994; no longer produced.

Perf.: $1300   **Exc.:** $1100   **VGood:** $800

Kimber Model 82C SuperAmerica Custom

Same specs as SuperAmerica except Neidner-style buttplate. Available options include: steel skeleton grip cap and buttplate; quarter-rib and open express sights; jewelled bolt; checkered bolt knob; special length of pull; rust blue finish. Reintroduced 1994.

Perf.: $1400   **Exc.:** $1200   **VGood:** $900

Kimber Model 82C Superclassic

Same specs as Model 82C except AAA Claro walnut stock with black rubber buttpad, as used on the SuperAmerica. Introduced 1995; no longer produced.

Perf.: $995   **Exc.:** $895   **VGood:** $695

Courtesy Kimber

KIMBER MODEL 84

Bolt action; 17 Rem., 17 Mach IV, 6x47, 5.6x50, 221 Rem. Fireball, 222 Rem. Mag., 222 Rem., 223 Rem.; 5-shot magazine; 22-inch barrel; 40½-inch overall length; weighs 6¼ lbs.; hooded ramp front sight with bead, folding leaf rear are optional; grooved for scope mounts; Claro walnut plain straight comb stock with hand-cut borderless checkering; steel grip cap; checkered steel buttplate; new Mauser-type head locking action; steel trigger guard; three-position safety (new in '87); hinged floorplate; Mauser-type extractor; fully-adjustable trigger. Introduced 1984; discontinued 1989.

Perf.: $950   **Exc.:** $795   **VGood:** $595

Kimber Model 84 Custom Classic Model

Same specs as Model 84 except select-grade Claro walnut stock with ebony forend tip, Neidner-style buttplate. Introduced 1984; discontinued 1988.

Perf.: $995   **Exc.:** $895   **VGood:** $695

Kimber Model 84 SuperAmerica

Same specs as Model 84 except 17 Rem., 221 Rem., 22 Hornet, 22-250, 222 Rem., 223 Rem., 250 Savage, 35 Rem.; 4-shot magazine; 22-inch barrel; detachable scope mounts; top-quality stock; right- or left-hand versions. Introduced 1985; discontinued 1988; reintroduced 1990; discontinued 1991.

Perf.: $1425   **Exc.:** $1095   **VGood:** $895

L.C. Smith

Syracuse, New York
Hunter Arms Company
Fulton, New York

Today:
Marlin Firearms Company
100 Kenna Drive
North Haven, Conn. 06473
Phone: *203-239-5621*
Website: *www.marlinfirearms.com*

    This brand represents one of the finest, most treasured commercial American-made double-barrel shotguns. The L.C. Smith shotguns were manufactured between 1880 and 1888 in Syracuse, New York, and between 1890 and 1945 in Fulton, New York, by the Hunter Arms Company. In 1945 Marlin Firearms acquired Hunter Arms and the L.C. Smith was made until 1951.

    In 1968 Marlin resurrected the line for five years, concluding in 1973.

    Today, Marlin has again resurrected the brand and is selling L.C. Smith shotguns from an offshore source.

Paul Goodwin photo

L.C. SMITH HAMMERLESS DOUBLE BARRELS (1913-1945)

Side-by-side; sidelock; hammerless; 10-, 12-, 16-, 20-ga., .410; 26-inch, 28-inch, 30-inch, 32-inch twist or fluid steel barrels; lowest grades stocked in American walnut, high grades in European walnut; straight-, half- or pistol-grip; splinter or beavertail forend. L.C. Smith guns built after 1912 follow the same basic specifications in gauges, barrel lengths, and other features as those made earlier. Their appearance is somewhat different, however, in that the frames and lockplates lack many of the complex, graceful curves and planes that characterize the older guns; this simpler, more straightforward shaping was an attempt by Hunter Arms to reduce the amount of milling and handwork that went into the guns, and thereby reduce the cost of manufacture. Beavertail forends became available in 1920; .410-bore guns in 1926; 10-ga. phased out in early 1920s; Featherweight frame available in some grades up to 1927, in all grades after 1927; special, extra-high solid rib available in all grades after 1939; manufactured by Hunter Arms Co., Fulton, New York. Introduced 1913; discontinued 1945.

..C. Smith Hammerless Double Barrel Field Grade (1913-1945)

Same specs as Hammerless Double Barrel (1913 to 1945), except 12-, 16-, 20-ga., .410; fluid steel barrels; American walnut pistol-grip stock; double triggers, extractors standard; single trigger, ejectors optional; a version featuring ivory sights and recoil pad was introduced in 1939 as the Field Special; total production, 141,844. Introduced 1913; discontinued 1945.

    Exc.: $995   **VGood:** $700   **Good:** $600

..C. Smith Hammerless Double Barrel Ideal Grade (1913-1945)

Same specs as Hammerless Double Barrel (1913 to 1945), except twist or fluid steel barrels; fluid steel barrels only, after 1917; 26-inch, 28-inch barrels only in .410; American walnut pistol-grip stock; straight or half-pistol grip optional; double triggers, extractors standard; single trigger, ejectors optional; total production, 21,862. Introduced 1913; discontinued 1945.

    Exc.: $1300   **VGood:** $900   **Good:** $800

..C. Smith Hammerless Double Barrel Specialty Grade (1913-1945)

Same specs as Hammerless Double Barrel (1913 to 1945), except fluid steel barrels standard; twist barrels optional until 1917; vent rib optional; American walnut straight-, half- or pistol-grip stock; double triggers, extractors standard; single trigger, ejectors optional; total production, 6,565. Introduced 1913; discontinued 1945.

    Exc.: $2000   **VGood:** $1400   **Good:** $1100

..C. Smith Hammerless Double Barrel Long Range Wild Fowl Gun 1913-1945)

Same specs as Hammerless Double Barrel (1913 to 1945), except 12-ga.; 3-inch chambers; 30-inch or 32-inch barrels; European walnut pistol-grip stock; straight- or pistol-grip optional; extractors or ejectors; double or single trigger; available in any standard grade. Introduced 1924; discontinued 1945.

    Exc.: $900   **VGood:** $600   **Good:** $500

Paul Goodwin photo

L.C. SMITH HAMMERLESS DOUBLE BARRELS (1945-1950)

Side-by-side; sidelock; hammerless; 10-, 12-, 16-, 20-ga., .410; 26-inch, 28-inch, 30-inch, 32-inch twist or fluid steel barrels; lowest grades stocked in American walnut, high grades in European walnut; straight-, half- or pistol-grip; splinter or beavertail forend. Marlin Firearms Company purchased Hunter Arms Company in 1945; guns built after 1945 were stamped L.C. SMITH GUN COMPANY; all grades of double gun except Field, Ideal, Specialty and Crown were discontinued; specifications for these grades remained same as before; manufactured by Marlin Firearms, Co. Introduced 1945; discontinued 1950.

L.C. Smith Hammerless Double Barrel Field Grade (1945-1950)

Same specs as Hammerless Double Barrel (1945 to 1950), except 12-, 16-, 20-ga., .410; fluid steel barrels; American walnut pistol-grip stock; double triggers, extractors standard; single trigger, ejectors optional; total production, 43,312. Introduced 1945; discontinued 1950.

Exc.: $900 **VGood:** $600 **Good:** $500

L.C. Smith Hammerless Double Barrel Ideal Grade (1945-1950)

Same specs as Hammerless Double Barrel (1945 to 1950), except fluid steel barrels; 26-inch, 28-inch barrels only in .410; American walnut pistol-grip stock; straight or half-pistol grip optional; double triggers, extractors standard; single trigger, ejectors optional; total production, 3950. Introduced 1945; discontinued 1950.

Exc.: $1300 **VGood:** $900 **Good:** $700

Paul Goodwin photo

L.C. SMITH SINGLE-BARREL TRAP GUN

Single shot; boxlock; hammerless; 12-ga.; 30-inch to 34-inch barrels (Olympic Grade 32-inch only); vent rib; hand-checkered American walnut pistol-grip stock, beavertail forend; ejectors; recoil pad; made in 10 grades with differing quality of workmanship, engraving and wood. Specialty, Eagle, Crown and Monogram grades introduced 1917; other grades introduced later (Olympic in 1928); Eagle Grade discontinued 1932; all others (except Olympic and Specialty) discontinued 1945; Olympic and Specialty grades discontinued 1950. Production totals as follows: Field Grade, 1; Ideal Grade, 5; Olympic Grade, 622; Specialty Grade, 1861; Trap Grade, 1; Eagle Grade, 56; Crown Grade, 88; Monogram Grade, 15; Premier Grade, 2; DeLuxe Grade, 3. The rarity of some grades precludes pricing.

Olympic Grade
Exc.: $1900   **VGood:** $1400   **Good:** $1000

Specialty Grade
Exc.: $2500   **VGood:** $1800   **Good:** $1400

Crown Grade
Exc.: $4500   **VGood:** $3000   **Good:** $2500

Monogram Grade
Exc.: $9000   **VGood:** $6000   **Good:** $5000

LEFEVER ARMS COMPANY

Syracuse, New York

This company was founded in 1884 by Dan Lefever, a pioneer in the field of breech-loading firearms. Over the years, he was responsible for many design improvements in the double-barrel shotgun, including the automatic hammerless system developed in the late 1880s. He also developed a compensating action that permitted adjustment for wear.

The Lefever was the first commercially successful double-barrel hammerless shotgun to be made in America.

In 1901 Lefever was forced out of his company and organized another, the D. M. Lefever, Sons & Company, also in Syracuse. Just a few years later, in 1906, Dan Lefever died and the new company went out of business.

In 1916, Ithaca acquired the original company and resumed production of the Lefever shotguns, producing them until 1948.

Paul Goodwin photo

LEFEVER NITRO SPECIAL

Side-by-side; boxlock; 12-, 16-, 20-ga., .410; 26-inch, 28-inch, 30-inch, 32-inch barrels; standard choke combos; hand-checkered American walnut pistol-grip stock, forearm; single nonselective trigger; optional double triggers; plain extractors. Introduced 1921; discontinued 1948.

With double triggers
Exc.: $440   **VGood:** $310   **Good:** $195

With single trigger
Exc.: $470   **VGood:** $350   **Good:** $250

NOTE: 16-gauge 20 percent higher; 20-gauge 50 percent higher than prices shown; .410, 200 percent higher.

Did You Know?

In 1883 LeFever patented the first truly automatic hammerless shotgun.

Marlin Firearms Company

100 Kenna Drive
North Haven, Conn. 06473
Phone: *203-239-5621*
Website: *www.marlinfirearms.com*

John M. Marlin was born in Connecticut in 1836, and served his apprenticeship as a tool and die maker. During the Civil War, he worked at the Colt plant in Hartford, and in 1870 hung out his sign on State Street, New Haven, manufacturing his own line of revolvers and derringers.

The young company developed enduring models, such as the Models 1891 and 1893. Today known as Models 39 and 336 respectively, they are the oldest shoulder arm designs in the world still being produced. The lever-action 22 repeater (now Model 39) became the favorite of many exhibition shooters, including the great Annie Oakley.

When John Marlin died in 1901, his two sons took over the business and began a diversification program. In 1915, during World War I, a New York syndicate bought the company and renamed it the Marlin Rockwell Corporation. After the War, the sporting firearms part of the business became a new corporation, which staggered until 1923, when it went on the auction block.

The story is told that the auction of the old Marlin Firearms operation in 1924 was attended by several curious children, a small dog and a lawyer named Frank Kenna. The Marlin Firearms Company has been owned and run by the Kennas ever since.

Thanks to an engineering philosophy seeking constant improvement, we have the first side-ejecting, solid-top receiver (called the "Marlin Safety") in 1889, the 1953 introduction of the micro-groove rifling system, and the 2004 introduction of the T-900 Fire Control System for bolt-action rimfire rifles.

In November of 2000, Marlin purchased the assets of H&R 1871, Inc., a Massachusetts-based manufacturer shotguns and rifles sold under the brand names of Harrington & Richardson and New England Firearms.

Founded in 1871, and today located in Gardner, Massachusetts, H&R 1871 markets its products under the brand names of Harrington & Richardson and New England Firearms. H&R 1871 is the largest manufacturer of single-shot shotguns and rifles in the world.

Marlin is best known for their classic long-lived lever-action rifles, such as the rimfire Model 39 and the centerfire Model 336. We all need a few Marlins in our gun rack.

Did You Know?

Marlin's philosophy has been to manufacture better products, even if it meant they were more expensive than the competitor's.

Paul Goodwin photo

MARLIN MODEL 94

Lever action; 25-20, 32-20, 38-40, 44-40; 10-shot magazine; 24-inch (standard), 15-inch, 20-inch, 26-inch, 28-inch, 30-inch, 32-inch round or octagonal barrel; solid frame or takedown; open rear, bead front sight; uncheckered pistol grip or straight stock, forearm. Originally marketed as Model 1894. Introduced 1894; discontinued 1933. Collector value.

Exc.: $1400   **VGood:** $895   **Good:** $695

Paul Goodwin photo

MARLIN MODEL 1894

Lever action; 41 Mag., 44 Mag., 45 Colt; 10-shot tube magazine; 20-inch carbine barrel; 37½-inch overall length; weighs 6 lbs.; hooded ramp front sight, semi-buckhorn adjustable rear; uncheckered straight grip black walnut stock, forearm; gold-plated trigger; receiver tapped for scope mount; offset hammer spur; solid top receiver sand blasted to reduce glare. 41 Mag. produced 1985-1988; 45 Colt produced 1989-1990. Introduced 1969; later production as Model 1894S.

Perf.: $300   **Exc.:** $270   **VGood:** $220

Marlin Model 1894C

Same specs as Model 1894 except 357 Mag.; 9-shot tube magazine; 18½-inch barrel; 35½-inch overall length; weighs 6 lbs. Introduced 1979; discontinued 1985. Improved version still offered.

Perf.: $380   **Exc.:** $290   **VGood:** $225

Paul Goodwin photo (old model)

MARLIN MODEL 95

Lever action; 33 WCF, 38-56, 40-65, 40-70, 40-82, 45-70; 9-shot tubular magazine; 24-inch round or octagonal barrel, other lengths on special order; open rear, bead front sight; uncheckered straight or pistol-grip stock, forearm. Originally marketed as Model 1895. Introduced 1895; discontinued 1915. Collector value.

Exc.: $2895   **VGood:** $2495   **Good:** $1700

Did You Know?

The standard Model 1895 weighed 8 lbs. and was offered with straight-wrist butts.

Courtesy Marlin (new model)

MARLIN MODEL 1895

Lever action; 45-70; 4-shot tube magazine; 22-inch round barrel; 40½-inch overall length; weighs 7 lbs.; offset hammer spur; adjustable semi-buckhorn folding rear sight, bead front; solid receiver tapped for scope mounts, receiver sights; two-piece uncheckered straight grip American walnut stock, forearm of black walnut; rubber buttplate; blued steel forend cap. Meant to be a recreation of the original Model 1895 discontinued in 1915. Actually built on action of Marlin Model 444. Introduced 1972; discontinued 1979. Updated version still in production.

Exc.: $350   **VGood:** $280   **Good:** $230

Marlin Model 1895S
Same specs as Model 1895 except full pistol-grip stock; straight buttpad. Introduced 1980; discontinued 1983.

Exc.: $300   **VGood:** $250   **Good:** $200

Marlin Model 1895SS
Same specs as Model 1895 except full pistol-grip stock; hammer-block safety. Introduced 1984; discontinued 2001.

Perf.: $350   **Exc.:** $290   **VGood:** $230

Paul Goodwin photo

MARLIN MODEL 36 RIFLE AND CARBINE

Lever action; 30-30, 32 Spl., 6-shot tube magazine, 20-inch (carbine), 24-inch (rifle) barrel, open rear sight, bead front; unchecked walnut pistol grip stock, semibeavertail forearm. Introduced in 1936, designation changed to Model 36 in 1937. Discontinued 1948.

> **Exc.:** $600   **VGood:** $400   **Good:** $325

Marlin Model 36-DL Deluxe Rifle

Lever action; 32 Spl., 30-30; 6-shot tubular magazine; 24-inch barrel; 42-inch overall length; weighs 6¾ lbs.; "Huntsmen" hooded ramp front sight with silver bead, flat-top rear; checkered American black walnut pistol-grip stock; semi-beavertail forearm; case-hardened receiver, lever; visible hammer; drilled, tapped for tang peep sight; detachable swivels; 1-inch leather sling. Introduced 1938; discontinued 1947.

> **Exc.:** $600   **VGood:** $450   **Good:** $325

Marlin Model 36-DL Carbine

Same specs as Model 36A except 20-inch barrel; 38-inch overall length; no checkering, swivels, sling.

> **Exc.:** $600   **VGood:** $450   **Good:** $325

Marlin Model 36RC

Same specs as Model 36 Carbine except "Huntsman" ramp front sight with silver bead and hood. Introduced 1938; discontinued 1947.

> **Exc.:** $600   **VGood:** $450   **VGood:** $325

Courtesy Marlin

MARLIN MODEL 336C

Lever-action; 30-30, 35 Rem., 32 Spl.; 6-shot tubular magazine; 20-inch barrel; 38½-inch overall length; weighs 7 lbs.; updated version of Model 36 carbine; semi-buckhorn adjustable folding rear sight, ramp front with Wide-Scan hood; receiver tapped for scope mounts; round breech bolt; gold-plated trigger; offset hammer spur; top of receiver sandblasted to reduce glare. Introduced 1948; discontinued 1983; updated version still in production.

Exc.: $270   **VGood:** $230   **Good:** $170

Courtesy Marlin

MARLIN MODEL 336A-DL

Same specs as Model 336C except 24-inch round barrel; two-thirds magazine tube; 6-shot; blued forearm cap; sling and sling swivels; hand-checkered stock, forearm. Discontinued 1962.

Exc.: $470   **VGood:** $370   **Good:** $290

Did You Know?

Tom Mix, an early silent Western movie star, used a lever-action Marlin .410 shotgun for trick shooting exhibitions.

Courtesy Marlin

MARLIN MODEL 336Y

Similar to Model 336C, but with 16½-inch barrel, short stock with 12½-inch length of pull; designed for young or smaller-stature hunters; 30-30 only.

Perf.: $500   **Exc.:** $400   **VGood:** n/a

Did You Know?

During her exhitibion shooting,
one of Annie Oakley's favorite guns
for trick shooting was a 22 caliber
Marlin Model 1897.

Paul Goodwin photo

MARLIN MODEL 39

Lever action; 22 Short, 22 Long, 22 LR; 18-shot (22 LR), 20-shot (22 Long), 25-shot (22 Short); 24-inch octagon barrel with tube magazine; open rear, bead front sight; uncheckered pistol-grip walnut stock, forearm. Introduced 1922; discontinued 1938.

Perf.: $1295   **Exc.:** $995   **VGood:** $450

Marlin Model 39A

Same specs as Model 39 except heavier stock; semi-beavertail forearm; semi-heavy round barrel. Introduced 1939; a version still remains in production. Early variations, better condition bring a premium.

Exc.: $400   **VGood:** $300   **Good:** $200

Marlin Model 39A Mountie

Same specs as Model 39A except 15-shot tubular magazine (22 LR), 16-shot (22 Long), 21-shot (22 Short); American black walnut straight-grip stock; slim forearm; 20-inch barrel; 36-inch overall length; weighs 6 lbs. Designation changed in 1972 to Model 39M. Introduced 1953; discontinued 1969.

Exc.: $250   **VGood:** $220   **Good:** $190

Marlin Model 39A Mountie Carbine

Same specs as Model 39A Mountie except weighs 5¼ lbs.; shorter tube magazine; 18-shot (22 Short, 14-shot (22 Long), 12-shot (22 LR).

Exc.: $250   **VGood:** $220   **Good:** $190

Marlin Model 39A

Same specs as Model 39 except 20-inch barrel; 36-inch overall length; weighs 6 lbs.; 21-shot (22 Short), 16-shot (22 Long), 15-shot (22 LR); straight-grip stock. Introduced 1963; discontinued 1987.

Exc.: $250   **VGood:** $220   **Good:** $190

Marlin Model 39A Octagon

Same specs as Model 39M except octagon barrel; bead front sight; hard rubber buttplate; squared lever. Introduced 1973.

Exc.: $650   **VGood:** $500   **Good:** $400

Courtesy Marlin

MARLIN MODEL 39A GOLDEN

Same specs as Model 39 except gold-plated trigger, other refinements. Introduced 1960. A version is still in production.

Perf.: $250   **Exc.:** $220   **VGood:** $190

Did You Know?

In addition to firearms, Marlin also produced razor blades in the 1930s.

Courtesy Marlin

MARLIN MODEL 783

Bolt action; 22 WMR; 13-shot tubular magazine; 22-inch barrel; 41-inch overall length; weighs 6 lbs.; open rear, ramp front sight; receiver grooved for scope mounts; select American walnut Monte Carlo stock; checkered pistol grip, forearm; white line spacer; gold-plated trigger; sling swivels; leather sling. Introduced 1971; discontinued 1988.

Exc.: $110   **VGood:** $95   **Good:** $80

Courtesy Marlin

MARLIN MODEL 99

Semi-automatic; 22 LR; 18-shot tube magazine; 22-inch barrel; 42-inch overall length; weighs 5½ lbs.; open rear, hooded ramp front sight; uncheckered walnut pistol-grip stock. Introduced 1959; discontinued 1961.

> **Exc.:** $100 **VGood:** $90 **Good:** $70

Marlin Model 99C *(shown)*

Same specs as Model 99 except uncheckered walnut pistol-grip stock with fluted comb; grooved receiver for tip-off scope mounts; gold-plated trigger. Later production features checkering on pistol grip, forearm. Introduced 1962; discontinued 1978.

> **Exc.:** $100 **VGood:** $90 **Good:** $80

Marlin Model 99DL

Same specs as Model 99 except for uncheckered black walnut Monte Carlo stock; jeweled bolt; gold-plated trigger; sling, sling swivels. Introduced 1960; discontinued 1965.

> **Exc.:** $110 **VGood:** $100 **Good:** $80

Marlin Model 99G

Same specs as Model 99C except plainer stock; bead front sight. Introduced 1960; discontinued 1965.

> **Exc.:** $100 **VGood:** $90 **Good:** $70

Marlin Model 99M1 Carbine

Same specs as Model 99C except designed after U.S. 30M1 carbine; 18-inch barrel; 37-inch overall length; weighs 4¾ lbs.; 10-shot tube magazine; uncheckered pistol grip carbine stock; handguard with barrel band; open rear, military-type ramp front sight; drilled, tapped for receiver sights; grooved for tip-off mount; gold-plated trigger; sling swivels. Introduced 1964; discontinued 1978.

> **Exc.:** $110 **VGood:** $100 **Good:** $90

Courtesy Marlin

MARLIN MODEL 989M2 CARBINE

Semi-automatic; 22 LR; 7-shot detachable clip magazine; 18-inch barrel; 37-inch overall length; weighs 4¾ lbs.; open rear sight, military-type ramp front; uncheckered pistol-grip carbine walnut stock and handguard; barrel band; sling swivels; gold-plated trigger. Introduced 1965; discontinued 1978.

Exc.: $110   **VGood:** $90   **Good:** $80

O. F. MOSSBERG & SONS, INC.

7 Grasso Avenue
North Haven, Connecticut 06473-3232
Phone: *203-230-5300*
Website: *www.mossberg.com*

This is America's oldest founding family-owned firearms manufacturer, founded in 1892 in Fitchburg, Massachusetts by Oscar F. Mossberg. In 1919, the company relocated to New Haven, Connecticut and finally settled permanently in North Haven, Connecticut in 1962.

Mossberg is well-known to today's shooter for its broad line of inexpensive but very functional shotguns. However, it wasn't too many years ago that Mossberg had lines of autoloading, pump- and lever-action 22 rimfire rifles, as well as their own bolt-action and lever-action centerfire rifles. From 1906 to 1940, Mossberg manufactured its only pistol, the Brownie, chambered for the 22 rimfire. This was an unusual pistol in that it had four barrels that were fired by a rotating firing pin.

For just a few years, in the mid-1970s, Mossberg opened the Pedersen Custom Gun Division and manufactured nicely finished centerfire bolt-action rifles and shotguns in slide-action, over/under and side-by-side designs. In the 1980s, Mossberg imported centerfire bolt-action rifles from Howa, in Japan.

Of particular interest are the 22 rimfire rifles made between the 1930s and 1970, and the centerfire rifles made up through the 1970s.

Paul Goodwin photo

MOSSBERG BROWNIE

Pocket pistol; top-break; double action; 22 LR, 22 Short; 4-shot; four 2½-inch barrels; revolving firing pin; steel extractor. Introduced in 1919; discontinued 1932.

Exc.: $325   **VGood:** $250   **Good:** $175

Did You Know?

The Brownie evolved from the Shattuck Unique, which was fired by squeezing the butt grip.

Courtesy Dixie Gunworks

MOSSBERG MODEL 42

Bolt action; 22 Short, 22 Long, 22 LR; 7-shot detachable box magazine; 24-inch barrel; takedown; receiver peep sight, open rear sight, hooded ramp front; uncheckered walnut pistol-grip stock; sling swivels. Introduced 1935; discontinued 1937.

Exc.: $100   **VGood:** $80   **Good:** $65

Mossberg Model 42A

Same specs as Model 42 with Master action, minor upgrading. Introduced 1937 to replace dropped Model 42; discontinued 1938.

Exc.: $110   **VGood:** $90   **Good:** $70

Mossberg Model L42A

Same specs as Model 42A except left-handed action. Introduced 1938; discontinued 1941.

Exc.: $135   **VGood:** $110   **Good:** $100

Mossberg Model 42B

Same specs as Model 42A except design improvements; replaced the Model 42A; micrometer peep sight in addition to open rear; 5-shot detachable box magazine. Introduced 1938; discontinued 1941.

Exc.: $110   **VGood:** $90   **Good:** $70

Mossberg Model 42M

Same specs as Model 42 except 23-inch tapered barrel; 40-inch overall length; weighs 6¾ lbs.; two-piece Mannlicher-type long stock with pistol grip, cheekpiece; micrometer receiver peep sight, open rear sight, hooded ramp front. Introduced 1940; discontinued 1950.

Exc.: $120   **VGood:** $100   **Good:** $75

Mossberg Model 42MB *(shown)*

Same same specs as Model 42M except no cheekpiece; approximately 50,000 made for U.S. and Great Britain; U.S. Property and British proofmarks. Produced only during World War II. Some collector value.

U.S. Property marked
Exc.: $175   **VGood:** $145   **Good:** $125

British proof marks
Exc.: $225   **VGood:** $195   **Good:** $165

Paul Goodwin photo

MOSSBERG MODEL 44US

Bolt action; 22 LR; 7-shot detachable box magazine; 26-inch heavy barrel; 43-inch overall length; weighs 8½ lbs.; same specs as Model 44B except designed primarily for teaching marksmanship to Armed Forces during World War II; uncheckered walnut target stock; sling swivels. Introduced 1943; discontinued 1948. Collector value.

Exc.: $200   **VGood:** $170   **Good:** $120

U.S. Property marked
Exc.: $210   **VGood:** $180   **Good:** $130

Mossberg Model 44US(a), 44US(b), 44US(c), 44US(d)
Same specs as Model 44US except minor changes in sights and extractors.

Exc.: $210   **VGood:** $180   **Good:** $130

Courtesy Dixie Gunworks

MOSSBERG MODEL 46

Bolt action; 22 Short, 22 Long, 22 LR; 15-shot (22 LR), 18-shot (22 Long), 22-shot (22 Short) tube magazine; 26-inch barrel; 44½-inch overall length; weighs 7½ lbs.; takedown repeater; micrometer rear peep sight; hooded ramp front; uncheckered walnut pistol-grip stock with cheekpiece; beavertail forearm; sling swivels. Introduced 1935; discontinued 1937.

Exc.: $110 **VGood:** $90 **Good:** $70

Mossberg Model 46A
Same specs as discontinued Model 46 with Master action and minor design improvements; detachable sling swivels. Introduced 1937; discontinued 1938.

Exc.: $120 **VGood:** $95 **Good:** $70

Mossberg Model 46AC
Same specs as Model 46A except open rear sight instead of micrometer peep sight.

Exc.: $100 **VGood:** $85 **Good:** $65

Mossberg Model 46A-LS
Same specs as Model 46A except equipped with factory-supplied Lyman No. 57 receiver sight.

Exc.: $150 **VGood:** $120 **Good:** $90

Mossberg Model 46M
Same specs as Model 46 except 23-inch barrel; 40-inch overall length; weighs 7 lbs.; micrometer receiver peep sight, open rear, hooded ramp front; two-piece Mannlicher-type stock with pistol grip, cheekpiece; sling swivels. Introduced 1940; discontinued 1952.

Exc.: $135 **VGood:** $110 **Good:** $80

Mossberg Model 46M(a), 46M(b) *(shown)*
Same specs as Model 46M except minor sight changes.

Exc.: $135 **VGood:** $110 **Good:** $80

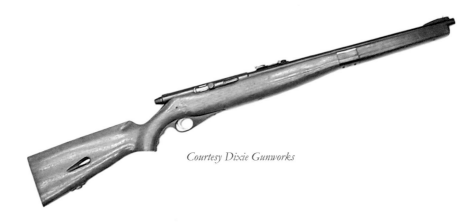

Courtesy Dixie Gunworks

MOSSBERG MODEL 51

Semi-automatic; 22 LR; 15-shot tube magazine; 24-inch barrel; 43¾-inch overall length; weighs 7¼ lbs.; receiver peep sight; sling swivels; cheekpiece stock; heavy beavertail forearm. Made only in 1939.

    Exc.: $150   **VGood:** $130   **Good:** $110

Mossberg Model 51M

Same specs as Model 51 except 20-inch round tapered barrel; 40-inch overall length; weighs 7 lbs.; two-piece Mannlicher-style stock. Introduced 1939; discontinued 1946.

    Exc.: $160   **VGood:** $130   **Good:** $100

Did You Know?

Mossberg was the first long-gun manufacturer in the U.S. to achieve ISO 9001 certification.

REMINGTON ARMS COMPANY, INC.

870 Remington Drive
P.O. Box 700
Madison, NC 27025-0700
Phone: *336-548-8700*
Website: *www.remington.com*

Founded in 1816 by Eliphalet Remington, a rifle barrel maker, today's Remington Arms Company can indeed claim to be the oldest firearms manufacturer (operating under the same name) in the United States today.

Although this company is well-known for its cap'n ball revolvers, single-shot rolling block rifles and early bolt-action sporting rifles, the early 1900s onward were years filled with interesting, well-made rifles and shotguns that are relatively plentiful today at affordable prices.

A perennial market leader in both rimfire and centerfire rifles as well as side-by-side, pump and autoloading shotguns, Remington has also been a preeminent name in target rifles—both rimfire and centerfire.

Like its peers, this company has had its ups and downs, and changed hands a few times—most recently in 1993. However, it has always operated under some version of the Remington name and has given the American sportsman such notable items as the Model 700 centerfire rifle and the Model 870 slide-action shotgun…and many other fine firearms that can be found in gunshops across the country.

Paul Goodwin photo

REMINGTON-LEE SPORTER

Bolt-action; 6mm USN, 30-30, 30-40, 303 British, 7mm Mauser, 7.65 Mauser, 32 Spl., 32-40, 35 Spl., 38-55, 38-72, 405 Win., 43 Spanish, 45-70, 45-90; 5-shot detachable box magazine; 24-inch, 26-inch barrel; open rear sight, bead front; hand-checkered American walnut pistol-grip stock. Collector value. Introduced 1886; discontinued 1906.

Exc.: $1550   **VGood:** $965   **Good:** $595

Remington-Lee Sporter Deluxe

Same specs as Remington-Lee Sporter except half-octagon barrel; Lyman sights; deluxe walnut stock. Collector value. Introduced 1886; discontinued 1906.

Exc.: $1795   **VGood:** $995   **Good:** $695

Courtesy Dixie Gunworks

REMINGTON NO. 6

Single shot; rolling block; 22 Short, 22 Long, 22 LR, 32 Rimfire Short, 32 Rimfire Long; 20-inch barrel; takedown; open front, rear sights; tang peep sight optional; plain straight stock, forearm. Introduced 1901; discontinued 1933.

Exc.: n/a   **VGood:** $625   **Good:** $350

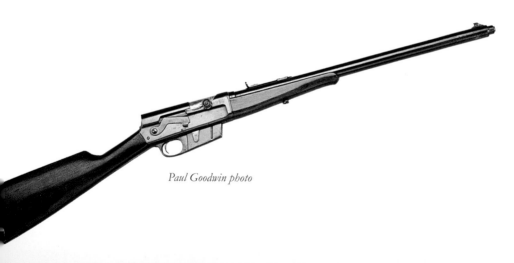

Paul Goodwin photo

REMINGTON MODEL 8, 8A

Semi-automatic; 25, 30, 32, 35 Rem.; 5-shot fixed box magazine; 22-inch barrel; bead front sight, open rear; plain walnut straight stock forearm. Introduced 1906; discontinued 1936.

Exc.: $525   **VGood:** $370   **Good:** $250

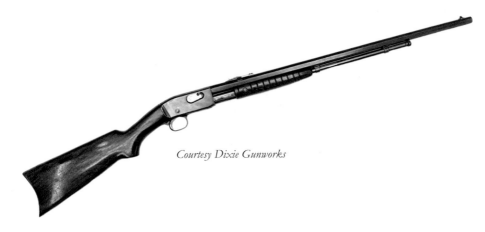

Courtesy Dixie Gunworks

REMINGTON MODEL 12, 12A

Slide action; 22 Short, 22 Long, 22 LR; 15-shot (22 Short), 12-shot (22 Long), 10-shot (22 LR) tube magazine; 22-inch barrel; hammerless takedown; bead front sight, open rear; uncheckered straight stock; grooved slide handle. Introduced 1909; discontinued 1936.

Exc.: $450   **VGood:** $350   **Good:** $300

Remington Model 12B
Same specs as Model 12A except 22 Short only; octagonal barrel.

Exc.: $475   **VGood:** $350   **Good:** $300

Courtesy Dixie Gunworks

Remington Model 12C
Slide action; 22 Short, 22 Long, 22 LR; 15-shot (22 Short), 12-shot (22 Long), 10-shot (22 LR) tube magazine; 24-inch octagonal barrel; hammerless takedown; bead front sight, open rear; uncheckered pistol-grip stock; grooved slide handle. Introduced 1909; discontinued 1936.

Exc.: $460   **VGood:** $385   **Good:** $315

Remington Model 12CS
Same specs as Model 12A except 22 Rem. Spl. (22 WRF); 12-shot magazine; 14-inch octagonal barrel; pistol-grip stock.

Exc.: $460   **VGood:** $360   **Good:** $310

Paul Goodwin photo

REMINGTON MODEL 24, 24A

Semi-automatic; 22 Short, 22 LR; 15-shot (22 Short), 10-shot (22 LR) tube magazine in buttstock; 21-inch barrel; takedown; bead front sight, open rear; uncheckered walnut stock, forearm. Introduced 1922; discontinued 1935.

Exc.: $380   **VGood:** $295   **Good:** $250

Courtesy Dixie Gunworks

REMINGTON MODEL 25, 25A

Slide action; 25-20, 32-20; 10-shot tube magazine; 24-inch barrel; hammerless; takedown; blade front sight, open rear; uncheckered walnut pistol-grip stock; grooved slide handle. Introduced 1923; discontinued 1936.

Exc.: $450   **VGood:** $345   **Good:** $300

Remington Model 25R Carbine

Same specs as Model 25A except 6-shot magazine; 18-inch barrel; straight stock.

Exc.: $520   **VGood:** $420   **Good:** $350

Paul Goodwin photo

REMINGTON MODEL 121A FIELDMASTER

Slide action; 22 Short, 22 Long, 22 LR; 20-shot (22 Short), 15-shot (22 Long), 14-shot (22 LR); 24-inch round barrel; weighs 6 lbs.; hammerless; takedown; white metal bead ramp front sights, step-adjustable rear; uncheckered pistol-grip stock; grooved semi-beavertail slide handle. Introduced 1936; discontinued 1954.

Exc.: $445   **VGood:** $325   **Good:** $250

Remington Model 121S

Same specs as Model 121A except 22 Rem. Spl.; 12-shot magazine.

Exc.: $620   **VGood:** $430   **Good:** $335

Remington Model 121SB

Same specs as Model 121A except smoothbore barrel for 22 shot cartridge.

Exc.: $620   **VGood:** $500   **Good:** $400

Paul Goodwin photo

REMINGTON MODEL 141, 141A GAMEMASTER

Slide action; 30, 32, 35 Rem.; 5-shot tube magazine; 24-inch barrel; 42¾-inch overall length; weighs 7¾ lbs.; hammerless; takedown; white metal bead ramp front sight, step-adjustable rear; uncheckered American walnut half-pistol-grip stock; grooved slide handle. Introduced 1936; discontinued 1950.

Exc.: $470   **VGood:** $325   **Good:** $270

Remington Model 141R Carbine
Same specs as Model 141 except 30, 32 Rem., 18½-inch barrel.

Exc.: $490   **VGood:** $350   **Good:** $285

Did You Know?

In 1873, Remington also produced typewriters.

Paul Goodwin photo

REMINGTON MODEL 30A

Bolt action; 25, 30, 32, 35 Rem., 7mm Mauser, 30-06; 5-shot box magazine; early models with 24-inch barrel; military-type double-stage trigger; schnabel forearm tip; later versions with 22-inch barrel, checkered walnut stock forearm; uncheckered on earlier version with finger groove in forearm; pistol grip; bead front sight, open rear; modified commercial version of 1917 Enfield action. Introduced 1921; discontinued 1940.

Exc.: $450 **VGood:** $390 **Good:** $300

Remington Model 30R Carbine

Same specs as Model 30A except 20-inch barrel; plain stock.

Exc.: $550 **VGood:** $430 **Good:** $330

Remington Model 30S Sporting

Same specs as Model 30A except 25 Rem., 257 Roberts, 7mm Mauser, 30-06; 5-shot box magazine, 24-inch barrel; bead front sight, No. 48 Lyman receiver sight; long full forearm, high-comb checkered stock. Introduced 1930; discontinued 1940.

Exc.: $595 **VGood:** $495 **Good:** $375

Courtesy Dixie Gunworks

REMINGTON MODEL 33

Bolt action; single shot; 22 Short, 22 Long, 22 LR; 24-inch barrel; takedown; bead front sight, open rear; uncheckered pistol-grip stock; grooved forearm. Introduced 1931; discontinued 1936.

Exc.: $125   **VGood:** $100   **Good:** $75

Remington Model 33 NRA Junior

Same specs as Model 33 except Patridge front sight, Lyman peep-style rear; ⅞-inch sling; swivels.

Exc.: $185   **VGood:** $160   **Good:** $95

Did You Know?

Remington is the oldest firearms manufacturer in the United States.

Courtesy Dixie Gunworks

REMINGTON MODEL 41A TARGETMASTER

Bolt action; single shot; 22 Short, 22 Long, 22 LR; 27-inch barrel; takedown; bead front sight, open rear; uncheckered pistol-grip stock. Introduced 1936; discontinued 1940.

Exc.: $130   **VGood:** $110   **Good:** $90

Remington Model 41AS

Same specs as Model 41A Targetmaster except 22 Remington Special (22WRF) cartridge.

Exc.: $175   **Vgood:** $150   **Good:** $120

Remington Model 41P *(shown)*

Same specs as Model 41A Targetmaster except hooded front sight, peep-type rear.

Exc.: $140   **VGood:** $120   **Good:** $100

Remington Model 41SB

Same specs as Model 41A Targetmaster except smoothbore barrel for 22 shot cartridges.

Exc.: $230   **VGood:** $160   **Good:** $130

Courtesy Dixie Gunworks

REMINGTON MODEL 81, 81A WOODSMASTER

Semi-automatic; 30, 32, 35 Rem., 300 Savage; 5-shot non-detachable box magazine; 22-inch barrel; 41½-inch overall length; weighs 8 lbs.; white metal bead front sight, step-adjustable rear; takedown; hammerless; solid breech; uncheckered American walnut pistol-grip stock, forearm; shotgun-style buttplate. Introduced 1936 to replace Model 8; discontinued 1950.

Exc.: $425   **VGood:** $350   **Good:** $275

Did You Know?

In 1888, the company branched out and also produced sewing machines and cash registers.

Paul Goodwin photo

REMINGTON NYLON 66

Semi-automatic; 22 LR; 14-shot tube magazine in buttstock; 19½-inch barrel; 38½-inch overall length; weighs 4 lbs.; blade front sight, fully-adjustable open rear; receiver grooved for tip-off mounts; moulded nylon stock with checkered pistol grip, forearm; white diamond forend inlay; black pistol-grip cap; available in three stock colors: Seneca green, Mohawk brown and Apache black; latter has chrome-plated receiver cover. Introduced 1959; discontinued 1988.

Exc.: $250   **VGood:** $225   **Good:** $175

Paul Goodwin photo

REMINGTON MODEL 37 RANGEMASTER

Bolt action; 22 LR; 5-shot box magazine; single shot adapter supplied as standard; 28-inch heavy barrel; 46½-inch overall length; weighs 12 lbs.; Remington peep rear sight, hooded front; models available with Wittek Vaver or Marble-Goss receiver sight; scope bases; uncheckered target stock with or without sling; swivels. When introduced, barrel band held forward section of stock to barrel; with modification of forearm, barrel band eliminated in 1938. Introduced 1937; original version discontinued 1940.

    Exc.: $550   **VGood:** $470   **Good:** $400

Remington Model 37 Of 1940

Same specs as Model 37 except Miracle trigger mechanism; high-comb stock; beavertail forearm. Introduced 1940; discontinued 1954.

    Exc.: $650   **VGood:** $550   **Good:** $440

Paul Goodwin photo

REMINGTON MODEL 40X

Bolt action; single shot; 22 LR; 28-inch standard or heavy barrel; 46¾-inch overall length; weighs 12¾ lbs. (heavy barrel); Redfield Olympic sights optional; scope bases; American walnut, high comb target stock; built-in adjustable bedding device; adjustable swivel; rubber buttplate; action similar to Model 722; adjustable trigger. Introduced 1955; discontinued 1964.

Exc.: $575   **VGood:** $495   **Good:** $395

With sights
Exc.: $625   **VGood:** $530   **Good:** $450

Remington Model 40X Centerfire

Same specs as Model 40X except only 222 Rem., 222 Rem. Mag., 30-06, 308, other calibers on special request at additional cost. Introduced 1961; discontinued 1964.

Exc.: $550   **VGood:** $450   **Good:** $350

With sights
Exc.: $600   **VGood:** $530   **Good:** $430

Remington Model 40X Standard

Same specs as Model 40X except lighter standard-weight 28-inch barrel; weighs 10¾ lbs.

Exc.: $500   **VGood:** $400   **Good:** $300

With sights
Exc.: $550   **VGood:** $500   **Good:** $400

Remington

REMINGTON MODEL 40-XB RANGEMASTER RIMFIRE

Bolt action; single shot; 22 LR; 28-inch barrel, standard or heavyweight; 47-inch overall length; weighs 10¾ lbs. (standard barrel); no sights; American walnut target stock, with palm rest; adjustable swivel block on guide rail; adjustable trigger; rubber buttplate. Replaced Model 40X. Introduced 1964; discontinued 1974.

Exc.: $500 **VGood:** $400 **Good:** $350

Remington Model 40-XB Rangemaster Centerfire

Same specs as Model 40-XB Rangemaster except 222 Rem., 222 Rem. Mag., 223 Rem., 6mm, 7.62mm, 220 Swift, 243, 25-06, 7mm BR, 7mm Rem. Mag., 30-338, 300 Win. Mag., 30-06, 6mmx47, 6.5x55, 22-250, 244, 30-06, 308; stainless steel 27¼-inch barrel, standard or heavyweight; 47-inch overall length; weighs 11¼ lbs.; no sights; target stock; adjustable swivel block on guide rail; rubber buttplate. Introduced 1964; still in production.

Exc.: $1100 **VGood:** $825 **Good:** $650

Remington Model 40-XB Rangemaster Repeater

Same specs as Model 40-XB Rangemaster except repeater with 5-shot magazine. No longer in production.

Exc.: $1200 **VGood:** $925 **Good:** $740

Remington Model 40-XB Rangemaster Varmint Special KS

Same specs as Model 40-XB except single shot or repeater; 220 Swift; 27¼-inch stainless steel barrel; 45¾-inch overall length; weighs 9¾ lbs.; no sights; Kevlar aramid fiber stock; straight comb; cheekpiece; palm swell grip; black recoil pad; removable swivel studs; custom-built to order. Introduced 1987; discontinued 1990.

Perf.: $1195 **Exc.:** $895 **VGood:** $730

Remington

REMINGTON MODEL 40-XB-BR

Bolt action; single shot; 22 BR Rem., 222, 222 Rem. Mag., 223, 6mmx47, 6mm BR Rem., 7.62 NATO; stainless steel 20-inch light varmint, 26-inch heavy varmint barrel; 38-inch overall length (20-inch barrel); weighs 9¼ lbs.; no sights; supplied with scope blocks; select walnut stock; wide squared-off forend; adjustable trigger. Introduced 1978; discontinued 1989.

Perf.: $995   **Exc.:** $795   **VGood:** $650

Remington Model 40-XB-BR KS

Same specs as Model 40XB-BR except Kevlar stock. Introduced 1989; still in production.

Perf.: $1195   **Exc.:** $895   **VGood:** $730

Paul Goodwin photo

Remington Model 40-XR

Bolt-action; single-shot; 22 LR; 24-inch heavy target barrel; 42½-inch overall length; weighs 9¼ lbs.; no sights; drilled, tapped, furnished with scope blocks; American walnut position-style stock, with front swivel block, forend guide rail; adjustable buttplate; adjustable trigger. Meets ISU specs. Introduced 1975; discontinued 1991.

Exc.: $995 **VGood:** $850 **Good:** $695

Remington Model 40-XR Custom Sporter

Same specs as Model 40-XR except Custom Shop model; available in four grades. Duplicates Model 700 Centerfire rifle. Introduced 1986; discontinued 1991. Premium for higher grades.

Perf.: $1100 **Exc.:** $925 **VGood:** $795

Remington Model 40-XR KS

Same specs as Model 40-XR except 43½-inch overall length; weighs 10½ lbs.; Kevlar stock. Introduced 1989.

Exc.: $1150 **VGood:** $895 **Good:** $695

Remington Model 40-XR KS Sporter

Same specs as Model 40-XR except match chamber; Kevlar stock; special order only. Introduced 1994.

Exc.: $925 **VGood:** $680 **Good:** $535

Remington

REMINGTON MODEL 540XR

Bolt action; single shot; 22 LR; 26-inch medium-weight barrel; 43½-inch to 46¾-inch overall length; weighs 8⅞ lbs.; no sights; drilled, tapped for scope blocks; fitted with front sight base; Monte Carlo position-style stock; thumb groove, cheekpiece; adjustable buttplate; full-length guide rail; adjustable match trigger. Introduced 1974; discontinued 1983.

Exc.: $300   **VGood:** $250   **Good:** $220

Did You Know?

In 1926, Remington sold decorative patches with their logo.
This led to their clothing business, which they discontinued in 1995.

Paul Goodwin photo

REMINGTON MODEL 541S

Bolt action; 22 Short, 22 Long, 22 LR; 5-shot clip magazine; 24-inch barrel; 42⅝-inch overall length; weighs 5½ lbs.; no sights; drilled, tapped for scope mounts, receiver sights; American walnut Monte Carlo stock; checkered pistol grip, forearm; rosewood colored forend tip, pistol grip cap; checkered buttplate; thumb safety; engraved receiver, trigger guard. Introduced 1972; discontinued 1983.

Exc.: $400   **VGood:** $350   **Good:** $275

Did You Know?

The "Rattlesnake" was introduced in 1999. It was Remington's first endeavor into the knife industry.

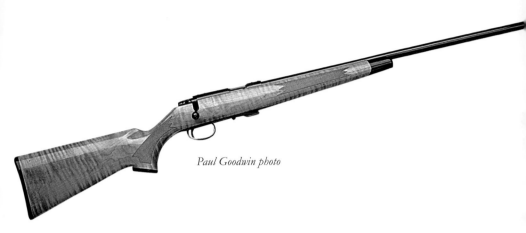

Paul Goodwin photo

REMINGTON MODEL 541T

Bolt action; 22 Short, 22 Long, 22 LR; 5-shot clip magazine; 24-inch barrel; 42⅝-inch overall length; weighs 5½ lbs.; no sights; drilled, tapped for scope mounts; American walnut Monte Carlo stock; checkered pistol grip, forearm; rosewood colored forend tip, pistol grip cap; checkered buttplate; thumb safety; satin finish. Introduced 1986.

Perf.: $350   **Exc.:** $275   **VGood:** $240

Remington Model 541T HB

Same specs as Model 541T except weighs about 6½ lbs; heavy target-type barrel without sights; receiver drilled and tapped for scope mounting; American walnut stock with straight comb, satin finish, cut checkering, black checkered buttplate, black grip cap and forend tip. Made in U.S. by Remington. Introduced 1993.

Perf.: $375   **Exc.:** $320   **VGood:** $280

REMINGTON MODEL 600

Bolt action; 222 Rem., 6mm Rem., 243, 308, 35 Rem.; 5-, 6-shot (222 Rem. only) magazine; 18½-inch round barrel with ventilated nylon rib; 37¼-inch overall length; weighs 5½ lbs.; blade ramp front sight, fully-adjustable open rear; drilled, tapped for scope mounts; checkered walnut Monte Carlo pistol-grip stock. Introduced 1964; discontinued 1967.

Exc.: $600 **VGood:** $475 **Good:** $375

223 Rem. (Rare)
Exc.: $650 **VGood:** $500 **Good:** $400

Remington Model 600 Magnum
Same specs as Model 600 except 6.5mm Rem. Mag., 350 Rem. Mag.; 4-shot box magazine; heavy Magnum-type barrel; weighs 6½ lbs.; laminated walnut/beech stock; recoil pad; swivels; sling. Introduced 1965; discontinued 1967.

Exc.: $800 **VGood:** $600 **Good:** $500

Remington Model 600 Mohawk
Same specs as Model 600 except 222 Rem., 6mm Rem., 243, 308; 18½-inch barrel with no rib; promotional model. Introduced 1971; discontinued 1980.

Exc.: $400 **VGood:** $325 **Good:** $250

Paul Goodwin photo

REMINGTON MODEL 700ADL

Bolt action; 222, 222 Rem. Mag., 22-250, 243, 25-06, 264 Win. Mag., 6mm Rem., 270, 280, 7mm Rem. Mag., 308, 30-06; 4-shot (264, 7mm), 6-shot (222, 222 Rem. Mag.), 5-shot (others); 20-inch, 22-inch, 24-inch round tapered barrel; 39½-inch overall length (222, 222 Rem. Mag., 243 Win.); removable, adjustable rear sight with windage screw, gold bead ramp front; tapped for scope mounts; walnut Monte Carlo stock, with pistol grip; originally introduced with hand-checkered pistol grip, forearm; made for several years with RKW finish, impressed checkering; more recent models with computerized cut checkering. Introduced 1962; still in production.

Perf.: $400 **Exc.:** $320 **VGood:** $285

With optional laminated stock
Perf.: $420 **Exc.:** $350 **VGood:** $300

Paul Goodwin photo

REMINGTON MODEL 700BDL

Bolt action; 17 Rem., 22-250, 222 Rem., 222 Rem. Mag., 243, 25-06, 264 Win. Mag., 270, 280, 300 Savage, 30-06, 308, 35 Whelen, 6mm Rem., 7mm Rem. Mag., 7mm-08, 300 Win. Mag., 338 Win. Mag., 8mm Mag.; 4-shot magazine; 20-inch, 22-inch, 24-inch barrel; stainless barrel (7mm Rem. Mag., 264, 300 Win. Mag.); with or without sights; select walnut, hand-checkered Monte Carlo stock; black forearm tip, pistol-grip cap, skip-line fleur-de-lis checkering; matted receiver top; quick-release floorplate; quick-detachable swivels, sling. Still in production.

Perf.: $465   **Exc.:** $400   **VGood:** $325

Left-hand model
Perf.: $545   **Exc.:** $470   **VGood:** $370

Paul Goodwin photo

Remington Model 700BDL Limited Classic

Same specs as Model 700BDL except made in classic style, with a different single chambering for each year; In sequence, from 1981 through 2005, the calibers were: 1981: 7x57, 1982: 257 Roberts., 1983: 300 H&H, 1984: 250-3000, 1985: 350 Rem Mag, 1986: 264 Win Mag, 1987: 338 Win Mag, 1988: 35 Whelen, 1989: 300 Wby Mag, 1990: 25-06, 1991: 7mm Wby Mag, 1992: 220 Swift, 1993: 222, 1994: 6.5x55, 1995: 300 Win Mag, 1996: 375 H&H, 1997: 280, 1998: 8mm Rem Mag, 1999: 17 Rem, 2000: 223, 2001: 7mm-08, 2002: 221 Fireball, 2003: 300 Savage, 2004: 8x57, 2005: 308; classic-style, hand-checkered walnut straight stock; black forearm tip, pistol-grip cap; high gloss blued finish. New caliber announced annually and produced for that year only. Introduced 1981; no longer in production.

Perf.: $635   **Exc.:** $480   **VGood:** $385

Paul Goodwin photo

REMINGTON MODEL 720A

Bolt action; 257 Roberts, 270, 30-06; 5-shot detachable box magazine; 22-inch barrel; 42½-inch overall length; weighs 8 lbs.; bead front sight on ramp, open rear; models available with Redfield No. 70RST micrometer or Lyman No. 48 receiver sights; checkered American walnut pistol-grip stock; modified Model 1917 Enfield action. Made only in 1941 as factory facilities were afterwards converted to wartime production. Note: Most 720s were made in 30-06; few in 270; and only a handful in 257 Roberts. Add premium for rarer calibers.

Exc.: $1250 **VGood:** $1000 **Good:** $700

Remington Model 720R

Same specs as Model 720A except 20-inch barrel; models available with Redfield No. 70RST micrometer or Lyman No. 48 receiver sights.

Exc.: $1250 **VGood:** $1000 **Good:** $700

Remington Model 720S

Same specs as Model 720A except 24-inch barrel; models available with Redfield No. 70RST micrometer or Lyman No. 48 receiver sights.

Exc.: $1250 **VGood:** $1000 **Good:** $700

Rock Island Auction photo

REMINGTON MODEL 721A

Bolt action; 270, 280, 30-06; 4-shot box magazine; 24-inch barrel; 44¼-inch overall length; weighs 7¼ lbs.; white metal bead front sight on ramp, step-adjustable sporting rear; uncheckered American walnut sporter stock with pistol grip; semi-beavertail forend; checkered shotgun-style buttplate; thumb safety; receiver drilled, tapped for scope mounts, micrometer sights. Introduced 1948; discontinued 1962.

Exc.: $300   **VGood:** $235   **Good:** $200

Did You Know?

The only difference between the Model 721 and Model 722 is action length.

Paul Goodwin photo

REMINGTON MODEL 722A

Bolt action, short action version of Model 721; 222 Rem., 222 Rem. Mag., 243 Win., 244 Rem., 257 Roberts, 300 Savage, 308; 4-, 5-shot (222 Rem.) magazine; 24-inch, 26-inch (222 Rem., 244 Rem.) barrel; 43¼-inch overall length; weighs 7 lbs.; shorter action than Model 721A; white metal bead front sight on ramp, step-adjustable sporting rear; receiver drilled, tapped for scope mounts or micrometer sights; uncheckered walnut sporter stock. Introduced 1948; discontinued 1962.

Exc.: $380   **VGood:** $310   **Good:** $275

Remington Model 722ADL

Same specs as Model 722A except deluxe checkered walnut sporter stock.

Exc.: $390   **VGood:** $320   **Good:** $285

Remington Model 722BDL

Same specs as Model 722A except select checkered walnut sporter stock.

Exc.: $450   **VGood:** $350   **Good:** $250

Paul Goodwin photo

REMINGTON MODEL 788

Bolt action; 222, 22-250, 223, 6mm Rem., 243, 7mm-08, 308, 30-30, 44 Mag.; 3-, 4-shot (222) detachable box magazine; 22-inch, 24-inch (222, 22-250) barrel; 41-inch to 43⅝-inch overall length; weighs 7-7½ lbs.; open fully-adjustable rear sight, blade ramp front; receiver tapped for scope mounts; American walnut or walnut-finished hardwood pistol-grip stock, uncheckered with Monte Carlo comb; thumb safety; artillery-type bolt. Introduced 1967; discontinued 1983.

Exc.: $360   **VGood:** $305   **Good:** $270

44 Mag., 7mm-08
Exc.: $415   **VGood:** $330   **Good:** $295

Remington Model 788 Carbine
Same specs as Model 788 except 18½-inch barrel.

Exc.: $370   **VGood:** $315   **Good:** $280

Remington Model 788 Left-Hand
Same specs as Model 788 except 6mm, 308; left-hand version. Introduced 1969.

Exc.: $375   **VGood:** $310   **Good:** $260

Remington

REMINGTON XP-100 CUSTOM HB LONG RANGE PISTOL

Single shot; bolt-action; 221 Rem. Fireball; 10½-inch barrel; 16¾-inch overall length; vent rib; blade front sight, adjustable rear; receiver drilled, tapped for scope mounts; one-piece brown nylon stock; blued finish. Introduced 1963; dropped 1985.

Exc.: $850   **VGood:** $700   **Good:** $575

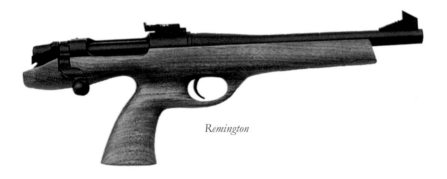

Remington

REMINGTON XP-100 SILHOUETTE

Single shot; bolt action; 7mm BR Rem.; 10½-inch barrel; 17¼-inch overall length; weighs 3⅞ lbs.; American walnut stock; blade front sight, fully-adjustable square-notch rear; mid-handle grip with scalloped contours for left- or right-handed use; match-type trigger; two-position thumb safety; matte blue finish. Dropped 1995.

Perf.: $500   **Exc.:** $400   **VGood:** $300

Remington

REMINGTON XP-100R KS

Single shot; bolt action; 223 Rem., 22-250, 7mm-08 Rem., 250 Savage, 308, 350 Rem. Mag., 35 Rem.; blind magazine; 5-shot (7mm-08, 35), 6-shot (223 Rem.); 14½-inch standard-weight barrel; weighs about 4½ lbs; rear-handle, synthetic Du Pont Kevlar stock to eliminate transfer bar between forward trigger and rear trigger assembly; front and rear sling swivel studs; adjustable leaf rear sight, bead front; receiver drilled and tapped for scope mounts. From Remington Custom Shop. Introduced 1990; dropped 1995.

New: $750   **Perf.:** $700   **Exc.:** $600

Paul Goodwin photo

REMINGTON MODEL 10A

Slide action; hammerless; takedown; 12-ga.; 6-shot tube magazine; 26-inch, 28-inch, 30-inch, 32-inch barrel; Full, Modified, Cylinder choke; uncheckered pistol-grip stock, grooved slide handle. Introduced 1907; discontinued 1929.

Exc.: $270   **VGood:** $195   **Good:** $170

Paul Goodwin photo

REMINGTON MODEL 17A

Slide action; hammerless; takedown; 26-inch, 28-inch, 30-inch, 32-inch barrel; plain barrel or solid rib; Modified, Full, Cylinder choke; uncheckered stock with pistol grip, grooved slide handle; Browning design. Introduced 1921; discontinued 1933.

Plain barrel
Exc.: $275   **VGood:** $220   **Good:** $195

Solid rib
Exc.: $375   **VGood:** $325   **Good:** $290

Paul Goodwin photo

REMINGTON MODEL 11A

Autoloader; hammerless; takedown; 12-, 16-, 20-ga.; 5-shot tube magazine; 26-inch, 28-inch, 30-inch, 32-inch barrel; Full, Modified, Improved Cylinder, Skeet chokes; plain, solid or vent rib; checkered pistol-grip stock, forearm. Introduced 1905; discontinued 1949.

Plain barrel
Exc.: $240   **VGood:** $215   **Good:** $185

Solid rib
Exc.: $315   **VGood:** $235   **Good:** $200

Vent rib
Exc.: $360   **VGood:** $335   **Good:** $305

Remington Model 11B Special
Same specs as Model 11A except higher grade of walnut, checkering and engraving. Discontinued 1948.
   Exc.: $440   **VGood:** $395   **Good:** $350

Remington Model 11D Tournament
Same specs as Model 11A except select grade of walnut, checkering and engraving. Discontinued 1948.
   Exc.: $850   **VGood:** $750   **Good:** $550

Remington Model 11E Expert
Same specs as Model 11A except fine grade of walnut, checkering and engraving. Discontinued 1948.
   Exc.: $975   **VGood:** $875   **Good:** $775

Remington Model 11F Premier
Same specs as Model 11A except best grade of walnut, checkering and engraving. Discontinued 1948.
   Exc.: $1550   **VGood:** $1375   **Good:** $1100

Remington Model 11R Riot Gun
Same specs as Model 11A except 12-ga.; special 20-inch barrel; sling swivels. Introduced 1921; discontinued 1948.
   Exc.: $300   **VGood:** $250   **Good:** $210

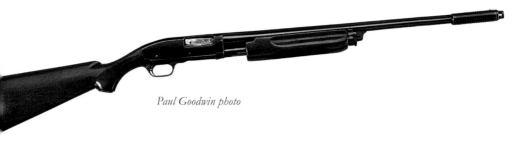

Paul Goodwin photo

REMINGTON MODEL 31A

Slide action; hammerless; takedown 12-, 16-, 20-ga.; 3-, 5-shot magazine; 26-inch, 28-inch, 30-inch, 32-inch barrel; plain barrel, solid or vent rib; Full, Modified, Improved Cylinder, Skeet choke; early models had checkered pistol-grip stock, slide handle; later styles had plain stock, grooved slide handle. Introduced 1931; discontinued 1949.

Plain barrel
Exc.: $345   **VGood:** $300   **Good:** $265

Solid rib
Exc.: $385   **VGood:** $345   **Good:** $300

Vent rib
Exc.: $415   **VGood:** $375   **Good:** $325

Remington Model 31B Special
Same specs as Model 31A except higher grade of wood, checkering and engraving. Introduced 1931; discontinued 1949.
Exc.: $550   **VGood:** $440   **Good:** $385

Remington Model 31D Tournament
Same specs as Model 31A except select grade of wood, checkering and engraving. Introduced 1931; discontinued 1949.
Exc.: $880   **VGood:** $715   **Good:** $550

Remington Model 31E Expert
Same specs as Model 31A except fine grade of wood, checkering and engraving. Introduced 1931; discontinued 1949.
Exc.: $935   **VGood:** $880   **Good:** $770

Remington Model 31F Premier
Same specs as Model 31A except best grade of wood, checkering and engraving. Introduced 1931; discontinued 1949.
Exc.: $1850   **VGood:** $1600   **Good:** $1500

Paul Goodwin photo

REMINGTON MODEL 11-48A

Autoloader; hammerless; takedown; 12-, 16-, 20-, 28-ga., .410; 4-, 5-shot tube magazine; 26-inch Improved Cylinder, 28-inch Modified or Full, 30-inch Full barrels; plain matted or vent-rib barrel; hand-checkered half-pistol-grip stock, forend; redesigned version of Model 11. Introduced 1949; discontinued 1969.

Plain barrel
Exc.: $300   **VGood:** $240   **Good:** $195

Vent-rib barrel
Exc.: $450   **VGood:** $350   **Good:** $300

Remington Model 11-48A Riot
Same specs as Model 11-48A except 12-ga.; 20-inch plain barrel. Introduced 1949; discontinued 1969.
Exc.: $300   **VGood:** $240   **Good:** $195

Remington Model 11-48B Special
Same specs as Model 11-48A except higher grade of wood, checkering and engraving. Introduced 1949; discontinued 1969.
Exc.: $325   **VGood:** $265   **Good:** $220

Remington Model 11-48D Tournament
Same specs as Model 11-48A except select grade of wood, checkering and engraving. Introduced 1949; discontinued 1969.
Exc.: $375   **VGood:** $300   **Good:** $260

Remington Model 11-48F Premier
Same specs as Model 11-48A except best grade of wood, checkering and engraving. Introduced 1949; discontinued 1969.
Exc.: $400   **VGood:** $320   **Good:** $280

Remington Model 11-48 RSS Slug Gun
Same specs as Model 11-48A except 12-ga. slug; 26-inch plain barrel; adjustable rifle-type gold bead front sight, step-adjustable rear. Introduced 1959; no longer in production.
Exc.: $350   **VGood:** $265   **Good:** $200

Remington Model 11-48SA Skeet
Same specs as Model 11-48A except 25-inch vent-rib barrel; Skeet choke; Skeet-style walnut stock, forend. Introduced 1952; discontinued 1969.
Exc.: $550   **VGood:** $480   **Good:** $400

Paul Goodwin photo

REMINGTON MODEL 11-87 PREMIER

Gas-operated autoloader; 12-ga.; 3-inch chamber; 26-inch, 28-inch, 30-inch vent-rib barrel; Rem-Choke tubes; weighs 8¼ lb.; metal bead middle sight, Bradley-type white-faced front; high-gloss or satin-finished, cut-checkered walnut stock, pinned forend; brown buttpad; pressure compensating system handles 2¾-inch or 3-inch shells; stainless steel magazine tube; barrel support ring on operating bars; left- or right-hand versions. Introduced, 1987; still in production.

Right-hand model
Perf.: $610   **Exc.:** $485   **VGood:** $410

Left-hand model
Perf.: $670   **Exc.:** $555   **VGood:** $475

Remington Model 11-87 Premier Skeet
Same specs as Model 11-87 Premier except 12-ga.; 2¾-inch chamber; 26-inch vent-rib barrel; cut-checkered, deluxe walnut Skeet-style stock with satin finish; two-piece buttplate. Introduced 1987; still in production.
Perf.: $650   **Exc.:** $550   **VGood:** $475

Remington Model 11-87 Premier Special Purpose Deer Gun
Same specs as Model 11-87 Premier except 21-inch barrel; rifled and Improved Cylinder choke tubes; rifle sights; cantilever scope mount, rings; gas system handles all 2¾-inch and 3-inch slug, buckshot, high-velocity field and magnum loads; not designed to function with light 2¾-inch field loads; dull stock finish, Parkerized exposed metal surfaces; bolt and carrier have blackened color. Introduced 1987; discontinued 1995.
Perf.: $690   **Exc.:** $495   **VGood:** $425

Paul Goodwin photo

Remington Model 11-87 Premier Special Purpose Magnum

Same specs as Model 11-87 Premier except black synthetic or satin wood stock; Parkerized metal finish; blackened bolt, carrier; quick-detachable sling swivels; camo padded nylon sling. Introduced 1987; still in production.

Perf.: $500 **Exc.:** $350 **VGood:** $260

With synthetic stock and forend (SPS).

Perf.: $610 **Exc.:** $475 **VGood:** $400

Remington Model 11-87 Premier Sporting Clays

Same specs as Model 11-87 Premier except 12-ga.; 2¾-inch chamber; 26-inch, 28-inch medium-height vent-rib Light Contour barrel; Skeet, Improved Cylinder, Modified, Full long Rem-Choke tubes; ivory bead front sight; special stock dimensions; shortened magazine tube and forend; Sporting Clays buttpad; lengthened forcing cone; competition trigger; top of receiver, barrel and rib matte finished; comes in two-barrel fitted hard case. Introduced 1992; still in production.

Perf.: $675 **Exc.:** $570 **VGood:** $450

Remington Model 11-87 Premier SPS Cantilever

Same specs as Model 11-87 Premier except 20-inch barrel; Improved Cylinder, 3½-inch rifled Rem-Choke tubes; cantilever scope mount; synthetic Monte Carlo stock; sling; swivels. Introduced 1994; still in production.

Perf.: $600 **Exc.:** $420 **VGood:** $320

Remington Model 11-87 Premier SPS-Deer

Same specs as Model 11-87 Premier except fully-rifled 21-inch barrel; rifle sights; black non-reflective synthetic stock, forend; black carrying sling. Introduced 1993; still in production.

Perf.: $525 **Exc.:** $375 **VGood:** $290

SAVAGE ARMS, INC.

118 Mountain Road
Suffield, Connecticut 06078
Phone: *413-568-7001*
Website: *www.savagearms.com*

Best known to today's collectors for its discontinued Model 99 lever-action centerfire rifle, Savage Arms was founded in 1894 in Utica, New York, by Arthur W. Savage. By 1915, the company was manufacturing both rimfire and centerfire rifles and pistols and supplied the Lewis machinegun during WWI.

In 1920, Savage purchased the J. Stevens Arms Company during the period of its association with the famous barrel-maker Harry Pope. A few years later, still in the '20s, the company acquired a number of businesses, including arms makers Crescent Firearms and the A. H. Fox company.

At around this point in its existence, Savage was reportedly the largest arms manufacturer in the free world.

During WWII, Savage/Stevens produced military small arms and machineguns. Later, in 1947, the sporting arms division moved to Chicopee Falls, Massachusetts, where it was amalgamated into the Stevens Arms Company. Like most of its arms-making peers, the company changed owners several times as well as shifting manufacturing locations.

In 1960, the entire operation was moved to Westfield, Massachusetts, where it remains today. In 1989 the company changed hands yet again, and remains under the same ownership to this day.

Savage made numerous models, in addition to the Model 99 lever-action rifle, that are of interest to us, including the Model 24 combo rifle/shotgun. These firearms, produced from the early 1900s up through the '70s, exhibit particularly good fit and finish.

Paul Goodwin photo

SAVAGE MODEL 99 (Original Version)

Lever action; 25-35, 30-30, 303 Savage, 32-40, 38-55; 5-shot rotary magazine; 22-inch (round), 26-inch (half, full octagon) barrel; hammerless; open rear sight, bead front; unchecked walnut straight-grip stock, tapered forearm. Introduced 1899; discontinued 1922.

Exc.: $1000   **VGood:** $800   **Good:** $495

Savage Model 99-358

Same specs as Model 99 except only 358 Win. caliber; grooved forend; recoil pad. Introduced 1977; discontinued 1980.

Exc.: $495   **VGood:** $400   **Good:** $310

Savage Model 99-375

Same specs as Model 99 except only 375 Win. caliber; recoil pad. Introduced 1980; discontinued 1980.

Exc.: $725   **VGood:** $605   **Good:** $475

Savage Model 99A (Early Model)

Same specs as Model 99 except 30-30, 300 Savage, 303 Savage; 24-inch or 26-inch barrel. Introduced 1920; discontinued 1936.

Exc.: $950   **VGood:** $700   **Good:** $500

Savage Model 99A (Late Model)

Same specs as Model 99 except 243, 250 Savage, 300 Savage, 308, 375 Win.; 20-inch, 22-inch barrel; 39¾-inch (20-inch barrel) overall length; weighs 7 lbs.; grooved trigger; straight walnut stock with Schnabel forend. Introduced 1971; discontinued 1981.

Exc.: $495   **VGood:** $450   **Good:** $350

Savage Model 99B

Same specs as original Model 99 except takedown design. Introduced 1922; discontinued 1936.

    Exc.: $925   **VGood:** $595   **Good:** $475

Savage Model 99C

Same specs as late-production Model 99 except detachable clip magazine replaces rotary type; 22-250, 243 Win., 284 Win., 308 Win. (284 dropped in 1974); 4-shot detachable magazine, 3-shot (284); 22-inch barrel; 41¾-inch overall length; weighs 6¾ lbs.; hammerless; solid breech; Damascened bolt; case-hardened lever; blue receiver; gold-plated trigger; top tang safety; hooded gold bead ramp front, adjustable folding ramp rear sight; receiver tapped for scope mounts; walnut stock with checkered pistol grip, forend; Monte Carlo comb; swivel studs. Introduced in 1965; last variation of the Model 99; production discontinued 1998.

    Exc.: $520   **VGood:** $430   **Good:** $370

Did You Know?

In 1992, Savage designed and patented the SNAIL, an environmentally friendly shooting range system. It was appropriately named because of its unique, patented circular deceleration chamber, minimizing lead pollution.

Courtesy Dixie Gunworks

SAVAGE MODEL 1903

Slide action; 22 Short, 22 Long, 22 LR; hammerless; takedown; detachable box magazine; 24-inch octagonal barrel; open rear sight, bead front; checkered one-piece pistol grip or straight stock. Introduced 1903; discontinued 1921.

Exc.: $270   **VGood:** $220   **Good:** $160

Did You Know?

Before developing firearms, Arthur Savage was owner of the largest cattle ranch in Australia.

Paul Goodwin photo

SAVAGE MODEL 1914

Slide action; 22 Short, 22 Long, 22 LR; 17-shot (22 LR) tubular magazine; 24-inch octagonal barrel; hammerless; takedown; open rear sight, bead front; uncheckered pistol-grip stock, grooved slide handle. Introduced 1914; discontinued 1924.

Exc.: $190   **VGood:** $150   **Good:** $100

Did You Know?

In 1919, Savage added the Indian head logo to the company name. It was a gift from Chief Lame Bear.

Courtesy Dixie Gunworks

SAVAGE MODEL 19

Bolt action; 22 LR; 5-shot detachable box magazine; 25-inch barrel; weighs 8 lbs.; early model with adjustable rear peep sight, blade front; later model with hooded front sight, Savage No. 15 fully-adjustable aperture extension rear; target-type uncheckered one-piece walnut stock; full pistol grip, 2-inch wide beavertail forearm; checkered buttplate; receiver drilled for scope blocks; 1¼-inch sling; sling swivels. Introduced 1933; discontinued 1946.

Exc.: $230   **VGood:** $190   **Good:** $150

Savage Model 19H
Same specs as Model 19 except chambered for 22 Hornet. Introduced 1933; discontinued 1942.

Exc.: $495   **VGood:** $440   **Good:** $300

Savage Model 19L
Same specs as Model 19 except Lyman 48Y receiver sight, No. 17A front sight. Introduced 1933; discontinued 1942.

Exc.: $325   **VGood:** $265   **Good:** $200

Savage Model 19M
Same specs as Model 19 except heavy 28-inch barrel; scope bases. Introduced 1933; discontinued 1942.

Exc.: $350   **VGood:** $290   **Good:** $220

Savage Model 19 NRA *(shown)*
Same specs as Model 19 except adjustable rear sight, blade front; American walnut military-type full stock, pistol grip; uncheckered. Introduced 1919; discontinued 1933.

Exc.: $230   **VGood:** $190   **Good:** $150

Courtesy Dixie Gunworks

SAVAGE MODEL 24

Over/under combo; 22 LR, 22 Short, 22 Long/410-3-inch or 2½-inch; 24-inch barrels; 40½-inch overall length; weighs 7 lbs.; takedown; barrel selection slide button on right side of receiver; full choke shotgun barrel; top-lever break-open; ramp front sight, elevation-adjustable rear; uncheckered walnut pistol-grip stock; visible hammer; single trigger; barrel selector on frame, later on hammer. Introduced 1950; discontinued 1965.

Exc.: $300   **VGood:** $275   **Good:** $200

Courtesy Dixie Gunworks

SAVAGE MODEL 25

Slide action; 22 Short, 22 Long, 22 LR; 20-shot (22 Short), 17-shot (22 Long), 15-shot (22 LR) tube magazine; 24-inch octagon barrel; hammerless; takedown; open rear sight, blade front; uncheckered American walnut pistol-grip stock; grooved slide handle. Introduced 1925; discontinued 1929.

Exc.: $290   **VGood:** $250   **Good:** $210

Did You Know?

At one time, Savage was the largest firearms manufacturing company in the Free World.

SAVAGE MODEL 30 STEVENS FAVORITE

Single shot, falling block; 22 LR, 22WMR 17 HMR; 20½-inch barrel; weighs 4.25 lbs.; 36.75-inch overall length; Walnut stock, straight grip, Schnabel forend; adjustable rear sight, bead post front. Lever-action falling block, inertia firing pin system, half octagonal or full octagonal bbl.

Perf.: $200   **Exc.:** $170   **VGood:** $140

Did You Know?

In 2000, Savage developed the world's first smokeless muzzleloader.

SMITH & WESSON

2100 Roosevelt Avenue
Springfield, Massachusetts 01104-1698
Phone: *413-781-8300*
Website: *www.smith-wesson.com*

The company we know today evolved from a failed early venture that produced the Volcanic lever-action cartridge-firing pistol, which in turn ultimately lead to the formation of the Winchester Repeating Arms Company. By that time, founders Horace Smith and Daniel B. Wesson had departed, relocating to Massachusetts in 1856 determined to manufacture a revolving cartridge-firing pistol.

Smith & Wesson went on to design and manufacture some of the finest revolvers ever produced. Their business faltered in the years following the Civil War, and the company went overseas searching for markets—and found them. Bolstered by the influx of overseas orders, the company invested in product development, with notable results. Among them, the new "top-break" revolver design that featured automatic ejection of fired brass to speed the unloading/reloading stage of the firing sequence.

Later, in 1880, the company introduced its first double-action revolvers. In 1899, S&W introduced what would become one of its most famous revolvers—the 38 Military and Police, the predecessor of the Model 10, designed to fire the new 38 S&W Special cartridge.

Going forward into the 1900s, we come into the era during which Smith & Wesson arguably made the best revolvers in the world, beginning with the Hand Ejector family.

The solid frame and swing-out cylinder of the hand ejector design opened the door to even more innovation and new designs. At this time, S&W introduced a growing family of frame sizes, labeling each with a letter of the alphabet. I/J frames were for the smallest revolvers in the 22-32 caliber range. K-frames handled the mid-size designs initially chambered for the more powerful 38 Special, but ultimately for everything from 22 rimfire to 357 Magnum. (Later, the slightly larger and stronger L-frame would appear on models intended for regular use of heavy loads, such as the 357 Magnum.) The N-frame was the largest, and used for the most powerful cartridges of the day, up to and including the 44 Magnum.

Smith & Wesson also made a few autoloading pistols in the 1930s, but it wasn't until the Model 41 target pistol arrived in 1957 that the company enjoyed commercial success with an autoloading pistol.

If you find a blued steel S&W in a dealer's showcase or on a gun show table, take a moment to look it over. It's a nice piece of machinery, and still affordable.

Did You Know?

History reports that Wyatt Earp used a Smith & Wesson Model No. 3 during the gunfight at the O.K. Corral in 1881.

Paul Goodwin photo

SMITH & WESSON SINGLE SHOT FIRST MODEL

Single shot; 22 LR, 32 S&W, 38 S&W; 6-inch, 8-inch, 10-inch barrels; target sights; square-butt, hard rubber grips; blued or nickel finish; built on same frame as 38 Single Action Third Model. Also furnished with 38 S&W barrel, cylinder to convert to single action. 1200 manufactured between 1893 and 1905; collector interest.

22 LR
Exc.: $650   **VGood:** $450   **Good:** $300

32 S&W
Exc.: $950   **VGood:** $650   **Good:** $350

38 S&W
Exc.: $900   **VGood:** $600   **Good:** $350

Smith & Wesson Single Shot Second Model

Same specs as First Model except 22 LR only; 10-inch barrel; cannot be converted to revolver configuration; serial numbered in separate series.
Exc.: $600   **VGood:** $450   **Good:** $275

Smith & Wesson Single Shot Third Model (Perfected Single Shot)

Same specs as First Model except 22 LR; hinged frame; target model; redesigned to incorporate new frame design developed for the 38 Double Action Perfected Model; checkered walnut target grips. Manufactured from 1909 to 1923. A special group featuring a short chamber was manufactured in 1910 and called the Olympic Model; the 22 LR cartridge must be forced into the rifling.
Exc.: $600   **VGood:** $450   **Good:** $300

Paul Goodwin photo

SMITH & WESSON MODEL 10 MILITARY & POLICE

Revolver; double action; 38 Spl.; 6-shot; 2-inch, 3-inch, 4-inch, 5-inch, 6½-inch barrel; 11⅛-inch overall length with square butt, ¼-inch less for round butt; weighs 31 oz.; ¹⁄₁₀-inch service-type front sight and square notch non-adjustable rear; square-butt checkered walnut stocks, round butt pattern with choice of hard rubber or checkered walnut; blued or nickel finish. In 1957 a 4-inch heavy barrel became available and is the 4-inch barrel configuration still available. The 38 M&P has been the true workhorse of the Smith & Wesson line of revolvers. The basic frame is termed S&W's K-frame, the derivative source of the K-38, et al. It is, quite possibly, the most popular, widely accepted police duty revolver ever made. Introduced about 1902. Reintroduced 1995.

Perf.: $250   **Exc.:** $200   **VGood:** $135

Nickel finish
Perf.: $275   **Exc.:** $225   **VGood:** $175

Smith & Wesson Model 10 Military & Police Heavy Barrel

Same specs as standard Model 10 except 4-inch heavy ribbed barrel; ramp front sight, square notch rear; square-butt; blued or nickel finish. Introduced 1957; still in production.

Perf.: $250   **Exc.:** $200   **VGood:** $150

Paul Goodwin photo

SMITH & WESSON 44 HAND EJECTOR 1ST MODEL

Revolver; 44 S&W Spl., 44 S&W Russian, 44-40, 45 Colt, 45 S&W Spl., 450 Eley, 455 Mark II; 6-shot cylinder; 4-inch, 5-inch, 6½-inch, 7½-inch barrel; also known as 44 Triple Lock and 44 New Century; square-butt checkered walnut grips; fixed or factory-fitted target sights. Introduced 1908; dropped 1915.

44 Russian, 44-40, 45 Colt, 45 S&W Spl., 450 Eley
Exc.: $1600   **VGood:** $1100   **Good:** $700

44 S&W Special
Exc.: $1250   **VGood:** $800   **Good:** $500

455 Mark II
Exc.: $1000   **VGood:** $700   **Good:** $400

Paul Goodwin photo

SMITH & WESSON 22/32 TARGET

Revolver; 22 LR; 6-shot; 6-inch barrel; 10½-inch overall length; sights, ⅒-inch or ⅛-inch Patridge front, fully-adjustable square notch rear sight; stocks, special, oversize, square-butt pattern in checkered Circassian walnut with S&W monogram; chambers countersunk at the heads around 1935 for the higher-velocity cartridges; blued finish only. A forerunner of the Model 35. Introduced in 1911; superseded by the Model 35 in 1953.

Exc.: $600   **VGood:** $450   **Good:** $300

Paul Goodwin photo

SMITH & WESSON 44 HAND EJECTOR 2ND MODEL

Revolver; 44 S&W Special, 38-40, 44-40, 45 Colt; 4-inch, 5-inch, 6-inch, 6½-inch barrel; internal changes; on exterior, heavy barrel lug was dropped; cylinder size and frame cut enlarged; fixed or factory target sights. Introduced 1915; dropped 1937. Collector value.

44 S&W Special
Exc.: $450   **VGood:** $350   **Good:** $250

Other calibers
Exc.: $1500   **VGood:** $1200   **Good:** $600

Paul Goodwin photo

SMITH & WESSON 38 MILITARY & POLICE

Revolver; double action; 38 Spl.; 6-shot; 4-inch, 5-inch, 6-inch, 6½-inch barrels; hard rubber round butt (early models) or checkered walnut square-butt grips; blue or nickel finish. The first S&W K-frame was the 38 Hand Ejector which later became known as the 38 Military & Police. This model was introduced in 1899 and has been in continuous production. During the last 96 years, S&W has produced over 5 million of these revolvers, resulting in numerous variations which affect values only slightly. The most collectable of these, the 38 Hand Ejector First Model, can be easily recognized by the lack of a locking lug located on the underside of the barrel and the serial number 1 through 20,975. Between 1899 and 1940 this model was available with both fixed sights and an adjustable target sight. The target model, referred to as the 38 Military and Police Target Model, brings a premium price and was the predecessor to all K-frame target models.

38 Hand Ejector First Model
Exc.: $450   **VGood:** $300   **Good:** $150

Standard models
Exc.: $300   **VGood:** $225   **Good:** $135

Courtesy Dixie Gunworks

SMITH & WESSON 32 HAND EJECTOR (MODEL 30)

Revolver; double action; 32 S&W Long; will accept 32 S&W and 32 S&W Long wadcutter; 6-shot; 2-inch, 3-inch, 4-inch barrels; 6-inch available at one time; 8-inch overall length (4-inch barrel); weighs 18 oz.; checkered walnut grips with medallion; formerly hard rubber; serrated ramp front and square notch rear; blue or nickel finish. Introduced 1908; dropped 1972.

Exc.: $250   **VGood:** $150   **Good:** $110

Did You Know?

In the mid-1800s, the first Smith & Wesson company was sold to a shirt manufacturing company owned by Oliver Winchester.

Paul Goodwin photo

SMITH & WESSON MODEL 35

Semi-automatic; 35 S&W Auto; 7-shot magazine; 3½-inch barrel; 6½-inch overall length; uncheckered walnut stocks; fixed sights; blued or nickel finish. Manufactured 1913 to 1921. Collector interest.

Exc.: $500   **VGood:** $375   **Good:** $250

Paul Goodwin photo

SMITH & WESSON MILITARY MODEL OF 1917

Revolver; 45 ACP, 45 Auto Rim. Entry of the U.S. into WWI found facilities unable to produce sufficient quantities of the recently adopted Colt Government Model auto pistol, so approximately 175,000 Smith & Wesson revolvers were manufactured, being chambered to fire the 45 ACP cartridge by means of the two 3-shot steel clips; also fires the 45 Auto Rim round. The wartime units had a duller blued finish and smooth walnut grips, with 5½-inch barrel; overall length, 10¼-inch; weighs 36¼ oz. with lanyard ring in the butt. A commercial version remained in production after the end of WWI to the start of WWII, distinguished by a bright blue finish and checkered walnut stocks.

Military model
Exc.: $550   **VGood:** $400   **Good:** $300

Commercial model
Exc.: $500   **VGood:** $300   **Good:** $250

Paul Goodwin photo

SMITH & WESSON MODEL 32 AUTO

Semi-automatic; 32 ACP, 7.65mm; 8-shot; 4-inch barrel; 7-inch overall length; weighs 28 oz.; unusual grip safety just below the trigger guard; successor to S&W's original auto pistol; walnut, uncheckered grips; blue or nickel finish. Introduced 1924; discontinued 1937. Collector interest.

Exc.: $2500   **VGood:** $2000   **Good:** $1500

Paul Goodwin photo

SMITH & WESSON K-22 OUTDOORSMAN

Revolver; 22 LR; 6-shot; 6-inch round barrel; adjustable rear sight; square-butt checkered walnut grips; blue finish. Also known as the K-22 First Model, this was the first in a long line of K-frame 22 rimfire target revolvers. Introduced 1931.

Exc.: $450   **VGood:** $300   **Good:** $200

Paul Goodwin photo

SMITH & WESSON K-22 SECOND MODEL

Revolver; 22 LR; 6-shot; 6-inch round barrel; checkered walnut square-butt grips; blue finish. This revolver was the first to be called the "Masterpiece." It was introduced in 1940 and, because of the factory shift to wartime production, it was manufactured for only a limited time. Total production was 1067 revolvers in serial number range 682,420 to 696,952 without a letter prefix.

Exc.: $1000   **VGood:** $850   **Good:** $500

Paul Goodwin photo

SMITH & WESSON K-32 FIRST MODEL

Revolver; 32 S&W Long; 6-inch round barrel; checkered walnut square-butt grips; blue finish. The K-32 First Model was a companion model to both the 38 M&P and K-22 Outdoorsman. It was introduced in 1938 and only produced until 1940 with approximately 125 handguns manufactured. It is the rarest of the early target models.

Exc.: $3000   **VGood:** $2500   **Good:** $1800

Paul Goodwin photo

SMITH & WESSON MODEL 14 K-38 MASTERPIECE

Revolver; double action; 38 Spl.; 6-shot; 6-inch, 8⅜-inch barrel; 11⅛-inch overall length (6-inch barrel); swing-out cylinder; micrometer rear sight, ⅛-inch Patridge-type front; hand-checkered service-type walnut grips; blued. Introduced 1947; dropped 1983.

Exc.: $250   **VGood:** $200   **Good:** $150

Smith & Wesson Model 14 K-38 Masterpiece Full Lug

Same specs as standard Model 14 except 6-inch full-lug barrel; weighs 47 oz.; pinned Patridge-type front sight, micrometer click-adjustable rear; square-butt combat grips; combat trigger, hammer; polished blue finish. Reintroduced 1991; limited production.

New: $350   **Perf.:** $275   **Exc.:** $225

Smith & Wesson Model 14 K-38 Masterpiece Single Action

Same specs as standard Model 14 except 6-inch barrel only; single-action only; target hammer; target trigger.

Exc.: $275   **VGood:** $225   **Good:** $150

Paul Goodwin photo

SMITH & WESSON 38 MILITARY & POLICE VICTORY MODEL

Revolver; 38 Spl., 38 S&W; 2-inch, 4-inch, 5-inch barrels; smooth walnut grips; midnight black finish. The Victory Model is the WWII production variation of the 38 Military & Police Model. Its name was derived from the serial number prefix "V," a symbol for "Victory." The revolvers provided the U.S. government were in 38 Special; those provided to the U.S. Allied Forces in 38 S&W. At the end of WWII the "V" serial number prefix was changed to "S," which was continued to 1948 when the series again reached 1,000,000. Add 50 percent for U.S. military markings (beware of fakes!).

Exc.: $300   **VGood:** $200   **Good:** $125

Paul Goodwin photo

SMITH & WESSON MODEL 15 38 COMBAT MASTERPIECE

Revolver; double action; 38 Spl.; 6-shot; 2-inch, 4-inch, 6-inch, 8⅜-inch barrel; 9⅛-inch overall length; weighs 34 oz.; blue or nickel finish. It took some years after WWII to re-establish commercial production and begin catching up with civilian demands at S&W. By the early '50s the situation was bright enough to warrant introducing a 4-inch version of the K-38, which was designated the 38 Combat Masterpiece. Its only nominal companion was the 22 Combat Masterpiece and no attempt was made to match loaded weights, as in the K-series-the 38 weighing 34 oz. empty, compared to 36½ oz. for the 22 version. Barrel ribs were narrower than the K-series and front sights were of the Baughman, quick-draw ramp pattern, replacing the vertical surface of the K-series Patridge-type. No longer in production.

New: $350   **Perf.:** $275   **Exc.:** $200

Nickel finish
New: $375   **Perf.:** $300   **Exc.:** $250

Paul Goodwin photos

SMITH & WESSON MODEL 17 K-22 MASTERPIECE

Revolver; double action; 22 LR; 6-shot; 6-inch barrel standard, 8⅜-inch available; 11⅛-inch overall length (6-inch barrel); weighs 38½ oz. (6-inch), 42½ oz. (8⅜-inch) loaded; blue finish. Redesigned version of Model 16. Postwar production added the refinement of a broad barrel rib, intended to compensate for weight variations between the three Masterpiece models. Likewise added were the redesigned hammer with its broad spur and thumb tip relief notch, an adjustable anti-backlash stop for the trigger and the Magna-type grips developed in the mid-'30s to help cushion the recoil of the 357 Magnum. Introduced around 1947; dropped 1998.

6-inch barrel
Perf.: $300   **Exc.:** $250   **VGood:** $200

8⅜-inch barrel
Perf.: $350   **Exc.:** $300   **VGood:** $250

Paul Goodwin photo

SMITH & WESSON MODEL 18 22 COMBAT MASTERPIECE

Revolver; double action; 22 LR, 22 Long, 22 Short; 6-shot; 4-inch barrel; 9⅛-inch overall length; weighs 36½ oz. (loaded); Baughman ⅛-inch quick-draw front sight on plain ramp, fully-adjustable S&W micrometer-click rear; checkered walnut, Magna-type grips with S&W medallion; options include broad-spur target hammer, wide target trigger, hand-filling target stocks, red front sight insert and white outlined rear sight notch; finish, blue only. Dropped 1985.

Exc.: $275 **VGood:** $250 **Good:** $200

Did You Know?

In 1935, the first magnum revolver,
the 357 Magnum,
was introduced by Smith & Wesson.

Paul Goodwin photo

SMITH & WESSON MODEL 19 COMBAT MAGNUM

Revolver; double action; 357 Mag.; 6-shot; 2½-inch, 4-inch, 6-inch barrel; available with 4-inch barrel; 9½-inch overall length; weighs 35 oz.; ⅛-inch Baughman quick-draw front plain ramp, fully-adjustable S&W micrometer-click rear; checkered Goncalo Alves grips with S&W medallion; S&W bright blue or nickel finish; built on the lighter S&W K-frame as used on the K-38, et al., rather than on the heavier N-frame used for the Model 27 and 28. Introduced about 1956; dropped 1999.

New: $350   **Perf.:** $300   **Exc.:** $225

Paul Goodwin photo

SMITH & WESSON 38/44 HEAVY DUTY (MODEL 20)

Revolver; 38 Spl.; 6-shot; 4-inch, 5-inch, 6½-inch barrel; 10⅜-inch overall length (5-inch barrel); weighs 40 oz.; built on the S&W 44 frame, often termed N-frame, hence the 38/44 designation; designed to handle high-velocity 38 Special ammunition; fixed sights, with ¹/₁₀-inch service-type (semi-circle) front and square notch rear; checkered walnut Magna-type grips with S&W medallion; blued or nickel finish. Introduced 1930; discontinued 1967.

Pre-War
Exc.: $550   **VGood:** $400   **Good:** $250

Post-War
Exc.: $300   **VGood:** $225   **Good:** $150

Paul Goodwin photo

SMITH & WESSON 38/44 OUTDOORSMAN (MODEL 23)

Revolver; 38 Spl.; 6-shot; 6½-inch barrel; 11¾-inch overall length; weighs, 41¾ oz.; plain Patridge ⅛-inch front sight, S&W micro-adjustable rear; blue finish. Introduced in 1930 as a companion to the Model 20; reintroduced about 1950 with ribbed barrel and Magna-type stocks. Discontinued 1967.

Pre-War
Exc.: $800   **VGood:** $600   **Good:** $400

Post-War
Exc.: $500   **VGood:** $400   **Good:** $300

Paul Goodwin photo

SMITH & WESSON 22/32 KIT GUN

Revolver; 22 LR; 6-shot; 4-inch barrel; 8-inch overall length; weighs 21 oz.; $\frac{1}{10}$-inch Patridge or pocket revolver front sight, with rear sight adjustable for elevation and windage; checkered round-butt Circassian walnut or hard rubber stocks; (small or special oversized target square-butt stocks were offered on special order); blued or nickel finish; a compact outdoorsman's revolver based on the 22/32 Target. Introduced in 1935; replaced in 1953 by the Model 34.

Exc.: $750   **VGood:** $500   **Good:** $400

Paul Goodwin photo

SMITH & WESSON MODEL 25

Revolver; double action; 45 Colt; 6-shot cylinder; 4-inch, 6-inch, 8⅜-inch barrel; 11⅜-inch overall length (6-inch barrel); weighs about 46 oz.; target-type checkered Goncalo Alves grips; S&W red ramp front sight, S&W micrometer-click rear with white outline; available in bright blue or nickel finish; target trigger; target hammer. Dropped 1994.

4-inch or 6-inch barrel, blue
Perf.: $400   **Exc.:** $350   **VGood:** $300

8⅜-inch barrel, blue or nickel
Perf.: $450   **Exc.:** $400   **VGood:** $350

Paul Goodwin photo

SMITH & WESSON MODEL 25-5

Revolver; 45 Colt; 6-shot; 4-inch, 6-inch, 8⅜-inch barrel; adjustable sights; square-butt, checkered, target-type Goncalo Alves grips; blue or nickel finish. Introduced in 1978 and called the 25-5 to distinguish it from the Model 25-2 in 45 ACP. Available with presentation case. Discontinued 1987.

Exc.: $350   **VGood:** $300   **Good:** $250

Paul Goodwin photo

SMITH & WESSON MODEL 39 9MM AUTO

Semi-automatic; 9mm; 8-shot magazine; 4-inch barrel; 7⁷⁄₁₆-inch overall length; weighs 26½ oz. sans magazine; ⅛-inch serrated ramp front, windage-adjustable square notch rear; checkered walnut grips with S&W medallion; bright blue or nickel finish. During the first dozen years of production, a limited number were made with steel frames rather than the standard aluminum alloy and command premium price. Introduced 1954. Collector value.

Exc.: $350   **VGood:** $250   **Good:** $175

Nickel finish
Exc.: $400   **VGood:** $275   **Good:** $200

Steel frame model
Exc.: $1100   **VGood:** $850   **Good:** $750

Paul Goodwin photo

SMITH & WESSON TERRIER (MODEL 32)

Revolver; 38 S&W, 38 Colt New Police; 5-shot; 2-inch barrel; 6¼-inch overall length; weighs 17 oz.; fixed sights with ⅒-inch serrated ramp front, square notch rear; round butt checkered walnut stocks with medallion; blue or nickel finish. Introduced 1936; dropped 1974.

Exc.: $250   **VGood:** $175   **Good:** $125

Rock Island Auction Company photo

SMITH & WESSON CHIEF'S SPECIAL (MODEL 36)

Revolver; double action; 38 Spl.; 5-shot; 2-inch, 3-inch barrel; 7⅜-inch overall length (3-inch barrel); weighs 21½ oz.; fixed 1/10-inch serrated front ramp, square notch rear; all steel frame and cylinder; checkered round butt soft rubber grips most common; square-butt available; blue or nickel finish. Dropped 1999.

New: $275   **Perf.:** $225   **Exc.:** $175

Paul Goodwin photo

SMITH & WESSON CHIEF'S SPECIAL AIRWEIGHT (MODEL 37)

Revolver; double action; 38 Spl.; 5-shot; 2-inch barrel; 6½-inch overall length; weighs 19½ oz.; lightweight version of Model 36, incorporating aluminum alloy frame; weighs 14½ oz.; fixed ¹⁄₁₀-inch serrated front ramp, square notch rear; all steel frame and cylinder; checkered round butt grips most common; square-butt available; blue or nickel finish. Still in production.

New: $350 **Perf.:** $275 **Exc.:** $225

Paul Goodwin photo

SMITH & WESSON CENTENNIAL (MODEL 40)

Revolver; double action; 38 Spl; 5-shot; 2-inch barrel; 6½-inch overall length; weighs 19 oz.; concealed hammer; fixed ¹⁄₁₀-inch serrated front ramp, square notch rear. Swing-out version of earlier top-break design with grip safety. Introduced 1953; dropped 1974. Collector value.

Exc.: $400   **VGood:** $350   **Good:** $275

Paul Goodwin photo

SMITH & WESSON 22 AUTO TARGET (MODEL 41)

Semi-automatic; 22 LR; 10-shot clip magazine; 5-inch, 7⅜-inch barrel; 12-inch overall length (7⅜-inch barrel); weighs 43½ oz.; ⅜-inch wide trigger, grooved, with adjustable stop; detachable muzzle brake supplied with 7⅜-inch barrel only (muzzle brake recently dropped); ⅛-inch undercut Patridge-type front sight, fully-adjustable S&W micrometer-click rear; checkered walnut grips with modified thumbrest for right- or left-handed shooters; S&W bright blue finish. The Model 41 was at one time also available in 22 Short for international competition. Introduced about 1957; still in production.

New: $650   **Perf.:** $600   **Exc.:** $500

Paul Goodwin photo

SMITH & WESSON 22 AUTO MATCH (MODEL 41)

Semi-automatic; 22 LR; 10-shot clip magazine; 5½-inch heavy barrel; 9-inch overall length; weighs 44½ oz.; checkered walnut stocks; modified thumbrest; ⅛-inch Patridge front sight on ramp base, S&W micro-click adjustable rear; grooved trigger; adjustable trigger stop; bright blued finish; matted top area. Extension front sight added 1965. Introduced 1963; dropped 1989.

Exc.: $750 **VGood:** $650 **Good:** $550

Did You Know?

In 1965 S&W began producing the world's first stainless steel revolver, the Model 60.

Paul Goodwin photo

SMITH & WESSON CENTENNIAL AIRWEIGHT (MODEL 42)

Revolver; double action; 38 Spl; 5-shot; 2-inch barrel; 6½-inch overall length; concealed hammer; aluminum alloy frame and cylinder; fixed ⅒-inch serrated front ramp, square notch rear. Lightweight version of Model 40. Introduced 1953; dropped 1974. Collector value.

Blue
Exc.: $400   **VGood:** $350   **Good:** $250

Nickel
Exc.: $950   **VGood:** $750   **Good:** $450

Paul Goodwin photo

SMITH & WESSON AIRWEIGHT KIT GUN (MODEL 43)

Revolver; 22 LR; 3½-inch barrel; 8-inch overall length; weighs 14¼-inch oz.; alloy aluminum frame and cylinder; fixed ⅟₁₀-inch serrated front ramp, micro-click adjustable rear; checkered walnut, round or square-butt stocks; blue or nickel finish. Introduced 1955; dropped 1974.

Exc.: $350   **VGood:** $300   **Good:** $250

Paul Goodwin photo

SMITH & WESSON BODYGUARD (MODEL 49)

Revolver; double action; 38 Spl.; 5-shot; 2-inch barrel; 6-5/16-inch overall length; steel construction; weighs 20½ oz.; fixed 1/10-inch serrated front ramp, square notch rear; blue or nickel finish; features shrouded hammer that can be cocked manually for single-action firing. Introduced 1955; dropped 1996.

Perf.: $250   **Exc.:** $200   **VGood:** $175

Paul Goodwin photo

SMITH & WESSON 1960 22/32 KIT GUN M.R.F. (MODEL 51)

Revolver; 22 WMR; 3½-inch barrel; 8-inch overall length; weighs 24 oz.; all steel frame and cylinder; fixed ¹⁄₁₀-inch serrated front ramp, micro-click adjustable rear; checkered walnut, round or square-butt stocks; blue or nickel finish. Introduced 1960; dropped 1974.

Exc.: $325   **VGood:** $275   **Good:** $225

Nickel finish
Exc.: $350   **VGood:** $300   **Good:** $250

Paul Goodwin photo

SMITH & WESSON 44 MAGNUM (MODEL 29)

Revolver; 44 Mag.; also handles 44 Spl., 44 Russian; 6-shot; 4-inch, 5-inch, 6½-inch, 8⅜-inch; 11⅞-inch overall length (6½-inch barrel); weighs 43 oz. (4-inch barrel), 47 oz. (6½-inch barrel), 51½ oz. (8⅜-inch barrel); ⅛-inch red ramp front sight, S&W micro-adjustable rear; target-type Goncalo Alves grips with S&W medallion; broad, grooved target trigger; wide-spur target hammer; bright blue or nickel finish. Introduced in 1956; still in production as Model 27 minus the cost-raising frills such as the checkered topstrap.

Exc.: $525   **VGood:** $375   **Good:** $250

Smith & Wesson 44 Magnum Model 29 Classic

Same specs as standard model except 5-inch, 6½-inch, 8⅜-inch barrel; chamfered cylinder front; interchangeable red ramp front, adjustable white outline rear sights; Hogue square-butt Santoprene grips; D&T for scope mount. Introduced 1990; no longer in production.

Exc.: $550   **VGood:** $450   **Good:** $375

Smith & Wesson 44 Magnum Model 29 Classic DX

Same specs as Model 29 Classic except 6½-inch, 8⅜-inch barrel with full-length lug; Morado combat-type grips. Five different front sight options and Hogue combat-style square butt conversion grip. Introduced 1991; no longer in production.

Exc.: $575   **VGood:** $475   **Good:** $375

Smith & Wesson 44 Magnum Model 29 Silhouette

Same specs as Model 29 except 10⅝-inch; oversize target-type checkered Goncalo Alves grips; four click-adjustable front sight positions. Introduced 1983; dropped 1991.

Exc.: $575   **VGood:** $475   **Good:** $375

Paul Goodwin photo

SMITH & WESSON 41 MAGNUM (MODEL 57)

Revolver; 41 Mag.; 6-shot; 4-inch, 6-inch, 8⅜-inch barrel; 11⅜-inch overall length (6-inch barrel); weighs 48 oz.; wide, grooved target trigger and broad-spur target hammer; ⅛-inch red ramp front, S&W micro-adjustable rear with white-outline notch; special oversize target-type of Goncalo Alves grips with S&W medallion; bright blue or nickel finish. Introduced as a deluxe companion to the Model 58, both being chambered for a new cartridge developed especially for them at that time, carrying a bullet of .410-inch diameter. The old 41 Long Colt cartridge cannot be fired in guns chambered for the 41 Magnum, nor can any other standard cartridge. Introduced 1964; dropped 1993.

> *4-inch and 6-inch barrels*
> **Perf.:** $300   **Exc.:** $250   **VGood:** $200
>
> *8⅜-inch barrel*
> **Perf.:** $325   **Exc.:** $275   **VGood:** $225

Paul Goodwin photo

SMITH & WESSON CHIEF'S SPECIAL STAINLESS (MODEL 60)

Revolver; double action; 38 Spl.; 5-shot; 2-inch barrel; 6½-inch overall length; weighs 19 oz.; stainless steel construction; fixed ¹⁄₁₀-inch serrated front ramp, square notch rear; checkered walnut round butt grips. Dropped 1996.

New: $300   **Perf.:** $250   **Exc.:** $225

Smith & Wesson Model 60 357 Magnum Chief's Special

Similar to the Model 60 in 38 Special except is 357 Magnum; 2⅛-inch or 3-inch barrel. Weighs 24 oz.; 7½-inch overall length (3-inch barrel). Has Uncle Mike's Combat grips.

New: $400   **Perf.:** $350   **Exc.:** $275

Paul Goodwin photo

SMITH & WESSON MODEL 64

Revolver; double action; 38 Spl.; 6-shot cylinder; 4-inch barrel; 9½-inch overall length; weighs 30½ oz.; Military & Police design; stainless steel construction; fixed, serrated front ramp sight, square-notch rear; service-style checkered American walnut square-butt stocks; satin finish. Introduced 1981; still in production.

Perf.: $325   **Exc.:** $275   **VGood:** $200

Paul Goodwin photo

SMITH & WESSON MODEL 66 COMBAT MAGNUM

Revolver; double action; 357 Mag., 38 Spl.; 6-shot cylinder; 2½-inch, 4-inch, 6-inch barrel; 9½-inch overall length (4-inch barrel); weighs 36 oz.; stainless steel construction; checkered Goncalo Alves target stocks; Baughman Quick Draw front sight on plain ramp, micro-click adjustable rear; grooved trigger, adjustable stop; satin finish. Introduced 1971; still in production.

Perf.: $375   **Exc.:** $325   **VGood:** $250

Paul Goodwin photo

SMITH & WESSON MODEL 65

Revolver; double action; 357 Mag.; 6-shot cylinder; 3-inch, 4-inch heavy barrel; 9⁵⁄₁₆-inch overall length (4-inch barrel); weighs 34 oz.; stainless steel construction; serrated ramp front sight, fixed square notch rear; square or round butt; blued finish. Introduced 1974; still in production.

Perf.: $350   **Exc.:** $275   **VGood:** $225

Smith & Wesson Model 65LS LadySmith

Same specs as the Model 65 except 3-inch barrel; weighs 31 oz.; rosewood round-butt grips; stainless steel construction with frosted finish; smooth combat trigger; service hammer; shrouded ejector rod; comes with soft case. Made in U.S. by Smith & Wesson. Introduced 1992; still produced.

New: $375   **Perf.:** $300   **Exc.:** $250

J. STEVENS ARMS COMPANY

(Savage Arms, Inc.)
118 Mountain Road
Suffield, Connecticut 06078
Phone: *413-568-7001*
Website: *www.savagearms.com*

This company opened its doors in 1864 under the name of J. Stevens and Company. Their first products were small single-shot pistols chambered for the 22- and 30-caliber rimfire cartridges of the day. In the latter 1800s, the first tip-up rifles were introduced, and subsequently Stevens moved from pistols into rifles, for which the company is best known.

In 1880 the business was incorporated as the J. Stevens Arms & Tool Company and operated as such until it was acquired by the Savage Arms Company in 1920. Stevens has been a division of Savage ever since.

Stevens produced a great many affordable firearms over the years, and many are collectible. The Stevens Favorite single-shot youth rifle, for example, was a simple, graceful rifle intended for young shooters. Over one million were made, in a number of variations, and you may encounter them just about any place at still-affordable prices.

Stevens also produced utility-grade side-by-side shotguns for over a century, ending in 1988. Single-shot shotguns were produced in great numbers, as well as utility-grade bolt- and slide-action shotguns that today have little if any collector interest—but there are lots of them out there, and most exhibit good fit and finish.

Courtesy Dixie Gunworks

STEVENS FAVORITE NO. 17

Lever action; single shot; 22 LR, 25 rimfire, 32 rimfire; 24-inch barrel, other lengths available on special order; takedown; open rear sight, Rocky Mountain front; uncheckered walnut straight-grip stock; tapered forearm. Introduced 1894; discontinued 1935. Collector value.

> **Exc.:** $270 **VGood:** $200 **Good:** $165

Courtesy Dixie Gunworks

STEVENS FAVORITE NO. 26 CRACKSHOT

Lever action; single shot; 22 LR, 32 rimfire; 18-inch, 22-inch barrel; takedown; open rear sight, blade front; uncheckered straight-grip walnut stock, tapered forearm. Introduced 1913; discontinued 1939. Collector value.

> **Exc.:** $220 **VGood:** $180 **Good:** $145

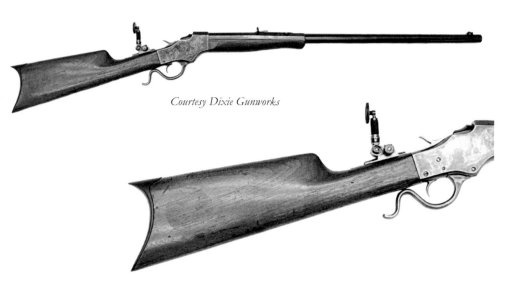

Courtesy Dixie Gunworks

STEVENS IDEAL NO. 44

Lever action; single shot; 22 LR, 25 rimfire, 32 rimfire, 25-20, 32-20, 32-40, 38-40, 38-55, 44-40; 24-inch, 26-inch round, full- or half-octagon barrel; rolling block; takedown; open rear sight, Rocky Mountain front; uncheckered straight-grip walnut stock, forearm. Introduced 1894; discontinued 1932. Primarily of collector interest.

Exc.: $685   **VGood:** $550   **Good:** $465

Did You Know?

Many Stevens guns did not have serial numbers, so they can only be "dated" to the period of production.

Courtesy Dixie Gunworks

STEVENS NO. 414 ARMORY MODEL

Lever action; single shot; 22 Short, 22 LR; 26-inch barrel; rolling block; Lyman receiver peep sight, blade front; checkered straight-grip walnut stock; military-style forearm; sling swivels. Introduced 1912; discontinued 1932.

Exc.: $600   **VGood:** $500   **Good:** $400

Courtesy Dixie Gunworks

STEVENS NO. 418 WALNUT HILL

Lever action; single shot; 22 Short, 22 LR; 26-inch barrel; takedown; Lyman No. 144 tang peep sight, blade front; unchecked walnut stock; pistol grip, semi-beavertail forearm; sling swivels, sling. Introduced 1932; discontinued 1940.

Exc.: $675   **VGood:** $495   **Good:** $300

Stevens No. 418½ Walnut Hill *(shown)*
Same specs as No. 418 Walnut Hill except 22 Short, 22 LR, 22 WRF, 25 Stevens; Lyman No. 2A tang peep sight, bead front. Introduced 1932; discontinued 1940.

Exc.: $695   **VGood:** $495   **Good:** $300

Courtesy Dixie Gunworks

STEVENS MODEL 94C

Single barrel; single shot; exposed hammer; break-open; early models side lever breaking; 12-, 16-, 20-ga., .410; 28-inch, 30-inch, 32-inch, 36-inch barrel; Full choke; checkered walnut finished hardwood pistol-grip stock, forearm; automatic ejector; color case-hardened frame. Introduced 1937; discontinued 1984.

    Perf.: $100   **Exc.:** $80   **VGood:** $60

Stevens Model 94Y

Same specs as Model 94C except top lever breaking; 20-ga., .410; 26-inch barrel; youth stock; recoil pad. Discontinued 1984.

    Perf.: $100   **Exc.:** $80   **VGood:** $60

Courtesy Dixie Gunworks

STEVENS MODEL 22-410

Over/under combo; exposed hammer; takedown; 22 Short, 22 Long, 22 LR barrel over .410 shotgun barrel; 24-inch barrels; Full choke; open rear sight, rifle-type ramp front; original models had uncheckered American walnut pistol-grip stock, forearm; later production had Tenite plastic stock, forearm; single trigger. Introduced 1938; discontinued 1950. Still in production by Savage Arms as Model 24, with variations.

With walnut stock
Exc.: $110   **VGood:** $90   **Good:** $70

With Tenite stock
Exc.: $145   **VGood:** $100   **Good:** $80

Courtesy Dixie Gunworks

STEVENS MODEL 240

Over/under; takedown; .410; 26-inch barrels; Full choke; early models had uncheckered American walnut pistol-grip stock, forearm; later versions had Tenite plastic stock forearm; double triggers. Introduced 1939; discontinued 1942.

With walnut stock
Exc.: $255   **VGood:** $190   **Good:** $170

With Tenite stock
Exc.: $270   **VGood:** $205   **Good:** $195

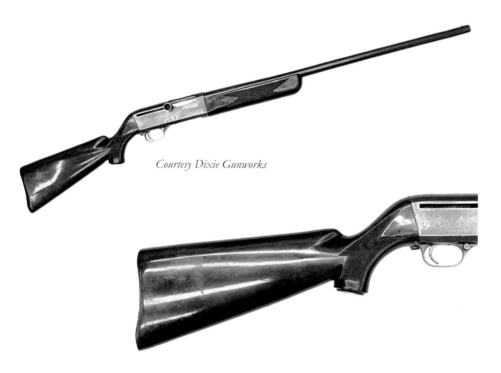

Courtesy Dixie Gunworks

STEVENS MODEL 124

Straight-pull bolt action; solid frame, hammerless; 12-ga.; 2-shot tube magazine; 28-inch barrel; Improved, Modified, Full chokes; checkered Tenite plastic stock, forearm. Introduced 1947; discontinued 1952.

Exc.: $175   **VGood:** $140   **Good:** $125

STEVENS/FOX

Savage Arms Company
Westfield, Massachusetts

The A. H. Fox Gun Company was established in Baltimore, Maryland, in 1896 by Ansley H. Fox. Early arms produced in his factory were made under the name of the Philadelphia Gun Company and 1905 he began operating under the name A.H. Fox.

In 1930, this company was purchased by the Savage Arms Company, which continued manufacturing all grades of Fox shotguns. Savage continued to produce the high-quality side-by-side shotguns until 1942 when they were dropped from the line. From 1942 onward, Savage made only the plainer grades of shotguns and marketed them under the Stevens brand.

The Stevens/Fox line of shotguns, less graceful in aspect, fit and finish than their predecessor A.H. Fox doubles, were nonetheless sturdily-made and represent a good opportunity for today's budget-minded shotgunner to add an American-made side-by-side shotgun to his gun rack.

Savage discontinued the Stevens/Fox shotguns beginning in the mid-1960s, leaving only the Model B-SE in production until 1987, when it too was dropped.

Paul Goodwin photo

STEVENS/FOX MODEL B

Side-by-side; boxlock; hammerless; 12-, 16-, 20-ga., .410; 26-inch, 28-inch, 30-inch barrels; Modified/Full, Improved/Modified, Full/Full chokes; hand-checkered American walnut pistol-grip stock, forearm; double triggers; plain extractors; case-hardened frame. Introduced 1940; no longer in production.

Exc.: $220   **VGood:** $170   **Good:** $125

Stevens/Fox Model B-DE

Same specs as Model B except for checkered select walnut pistol-grip stock, beavertail forearm; non-selective single trigger; satin chrome-finished frame; replaced Model B-DL. Introduced 1965; discontinued 1966.

Exc.: $240   **VGood:** $190   **Good:** $145

Stevens/Fox Model B-DL

Same specs as Model B except for checkered select walnut pistol-grip stock, beavertail forearm; non-selective single trigger; satin chrome-finished frame; sideplates. Introduced 1962; discontinued 1965.

Exc.: $230   **VGood:** $180   **Good:** $140

Stevens/Fox Model B-SE

Same specs as Model B except single trigger; selective ejectors. Introduced 1966; discontinued 1987.

Perf.: $400   **Exc.:** $310   **VGood:** $260

Stevens/Fox Model B-ST

Same specs as Model B except non-selective single trigger. Introduced 1955; discontinued 1966.

Exc.: $275   **VGood:** $200   **Good:** $120

Sturm, Ruger & Co., Inc.

1 Lacey Place
Southport, CT 06899
Phone: *203-259-7843*
Website: *www.ruger.com*

Founded in 1946 to produce and market an autoloading 22-rimfire pistol designed by William B. Ruger, this company is today the largest manufacturer of firearms in the United States. Bearing a strong resemblance to the Luger pistol familiar to returning veterans, the new Ruger 22 was a near-instant hit with Americans, and continues in production to the present day in the third model generation.

Within a few years, the company would introduce its first single-action revolver—the Single Six. At the time (1953), Western movies and television programming held the public interest and Colt had not yet resumed production of its iconic Single Action Army. So, a market vacuum existed, and this new single-action 22 dropped smoothly into it and the rest is history. Like the 22 autoloading pistol, the Single Six remains in production today following a variety of modifications and versions offered over the years.

With the success of the Single Six, in 1955 the company took the plunge into a larger single-action model, the Flattop. These first guns were chambered for the 357 Magnum cartridge. In 1956 Remington introduced a new pistol cartridge, the 44 Magnum, and Ruger was right there with a slightly larger revolver so chambered, the Blackhawk Flattop 44 Magnum. These guns were very successful and Ruger quickly expanded the line and continues to do so yet today.

Double-action revolvers were introduced in 1970, and became an important component of the company's business. Some years later, in 1987, Ruger introduced its first centerfire autoloading pistol, the P-85. Again successful, this pistol family continues in production today.

Arguably, the company is best known for its autoloading 22-rimfire rifle, the 10/22. Introduced in 1964, this rifle continues in production today and is perhaps the most customized commercial firearm on the market, its only real competition for that distinction being the 1911 pistol.

Centerfire rifles came along. In 1966, the No. 1 single-shot was offered in a growing variety of models and chamberings and continues in production to this day. The bolt-action Model 77 was introduced in 1968 and was immediately successful. A nice feature of this rifle is that the receiver is manufactured with integral scope bases (and mating 1-inch rings accompany each rifle), so mounting a scope was a relatively quick project. Nearly all the No.1 rifles were equipped with a quarter-rib that was also configured for the accompanying Ruger rings.

Shotguns came along in 1977 in the form of the 20-gauge Red Label over/under. The 12-gauge followed in 1982 and both models remain in production today, joined by new models and a 28-gauge chambering.

The earlier blued Ruger arms are increasingly sought by knowledgeable shooters and budding collectors. There's something about the smooth operational 'feel' of the pre-transfer bar single-action revolver, and the polished deep blue finish on the steel.

Paul Goodwin photo

STURM RUGER MARK I STANDARD MODEL

Semi-automatic; 22 LR only; 9-shot magazine 4¾-inch, 6-inch barrel (4¾-inch barrel), 8¾-inch overall length (6-inch barrel); checkered hard rubber grips walnut optional; windage-adjustable square-notch rear, fixed wide blade front sight; blued. Introduced 1949; dropped 1982 in favor of Mark II. Until 1951 featured red eagle insignia in grips; changed to black upon death of Alex Sturm. This type has considerable collector value.

Exc.: $150   **VGood:** $125   **Good:** $110

Red eagle model

Exc.: $350   **VGood:** $300   **Good:** $250

Sturm Ruger Mark I Target Model

Same specs as Standard Model except 5½-inch heavy barrel, 5¾-inch tapered barrel, 6⅞-inch heavy tapered barrel; adjustable rear, target front sight. Introduced 1951; dropped 1982.

Exc.: $175   **VGood:** $150   **Good:** $125

Paul Goodwin photo

STURM RUGER SINGLE-SIX

Revolver; single action; 22 LR, 22 WMR; 6-shot; 4⅝-inch, 5½-inch, 6½-inch, 9½-inch barrel; 10-inch overall length (4-inch barrel); checkered hard rubber grips on early production, uncheckered walnut on later versions; windage-adjustable rear sight; blued. Introduced 1953; dropped 1972.

Exc.: $200   **VGood:** $150   **Good:** $125

Sturm Ruger Single-Six Convertible

Same general specs as standard Single-Six except interchangeable cylinders, 22 LR, Long, Short/22 WRM; 5½-inch, 6½-inch, 9½-inch barrel. Introduced 1962; dropped 1972.

Exc.: $275   **VGood:** $225   **Good:** $185

Paul Goodwin photo

STURM RUGER BEARCAT (FIRST ISSUE)

Revolver; single action; 22 LR, 22 Long, 22 Short; 6-shot cylinder; 4-inch barrel; 8⅞-inch overall length; weighs 17 oz.; non-fluted cylinder; fixed Patridge front, square notch rear sights; alloy solid frame; uncheckered walnut grips; blued. Introduced 1958; dropped 1973.

Exc.: $300 **VGood:** $250 **Good:** $175

Sturm Ruger Bearcat (Second Issue) Super Bearcat

Revolver; single action; 22 LR, 22 Long, 22 Short; improved version of Bearcat except all-steel construction; weighs 22½ oz.; music wire coil springs; non-fluted engraved cylinder. Introduced 1971; dropped 1975.

Exc.: $275 **VGood:** $225 **Good:** $185

Paul Goodwin photo

STURM RUGER BLACKHAWK

Revolver; single action; 357 Mag., 41 Mag., 45 LC; 6-shot; 4⅝-inch, 6½-inch (357, 41 Mag.) barrel; 12-inch overall length (6½-inch barrel); large frame; checkered hard rubber or uncheckered walnut grips; hooded adjustable rear sight, ramp front; blued. Introduced 1965; dropped 1972.

New: $300 **Perf.:** $250 **Exc.:** $200

Sturm Ruger Blackhawk Convertible

Same specs as standard Blackhawk except interchangeable cylinders for 9mm Para., 357 Mag. or 45 Colt/45 ACP. Introduced 1967; dropped 1985.

Exc.: $435 **VGood:** $300 **Good:** $225

Paul Goodwin photo

STURM RUGER SUPER BLACKHAWK

Revolver; 44 Mag.; 5½-inch, 7½-inch, 10½-inch barrel; 13⅜-inch overall length (7½-inch barrel); weighs 48 oz.; ⅛-inch ramp front, micro-click fully-adjustable rear; American walnut grips; interlock mechanism; non-fluted cylinder; steel grip and cylinder frame; square back trigger guard; wide serrated trigger; wide spur hammer.

New: $519   **Perf.:** $350   **Exc.:** $250

Stainless
New: $535   **Perf.:** $370   **Exc.:** $300

Paul Goodwin photo

STURM RUGER BLACKHAWK NEW MODEL 357 MAXIMUM

Revolver; single action; 30 Carbine, 357 Maximum; 6-shot cylinder; 7½-inch, 10-inch bull barrel 16⅞-inch overall length (10½-inch barrel); weighs 42 oz.; new Ruger interlocked mechanism; transfer bar ignition; hardened chrome-moly steel frame; wide trigger music wire springs; independent firing pin; blue, stainless or high-gloss stainless finish. Introduced 1983; dropped 1984.

Exc.: $450   **VGood:** $375   **Good:** $300

Paul Goodwin photo

STURM RUGER REDHAWK

Revolver; double action; 41 Mag., 44 Mag.; 6-shot; 5½-inch, 7½-inch barrel; 5½-inch barrel added 1984; 13-inch overall length (7½-inch barrel); weighs 54 oz.; stainless steel brushed satin or blued finish; Patridge-type front sight, fully-adjustable rear; square-butt Goncalo Alves grips. Introduced 1979; still in production.

Blue
New: $585   **Perf.:** $475   **Exc.:** $300

Stainless
New: $645   **Perf.:** $450   **Exc.:** $350

Did You Know?

The Ruger Redhawk was the first double action revolver designed to endure the pressure of the powerful 44 Magnum cartridge.

Paul Goodwin photo

STURM RUGER MODEL 10/22 CARBINE

Semi-automatic; 22 LR; 10-shot detachable rotary magazine; 18½-inch barrel; uncheckered walnut carbine stock on early versions; as of 1980, standard models with birch stocks; barrel band; receiver tapped for scope blocks or tip-off mount; adjustable folding leaf rear sight, gold bead front; blue or stainless finish. Introduced 1964; still in production.

Perf.: $150   **Exc.:** $120   **VGood:** $100

Uncheckered walnut stock
Perf.: $185   **Exc.:** $145   **VGood:** $130

Stainless steel finish
Perf.: $220   **Exc.:** $185   **VGood:** $150

Sturm Ruger 10/22 Rifle

Same specs as 10/22 Carbine except 20-inch barrel, rifle stock with flat butt, no barrel band.

Perf.: $240   **Exc.:** $180   **VGood:** $120

Sturm Ruger Model 10/22 Sporter

Same specs as Model 10/22 except Monte Carlo stock with grooved forearm; grip cap; sling swivels. Dropped in 1971, but reintroduced in 1973, with hand-checkered walnut pistol-grip stock. Dropped 1975. Reintroduced, still in production. Premium for early model.

Exc.: $300   **VGood:** $270   **Good:** $190

Sturm Ruger 10/22t Target Rifle

Similar to the 10/22 except has 20-inch heavy, hammer-forged barrel with tight chamber dimensions, improved trigger pull, laminated hardwood stock dimensioned for optical sights; no iron sights supplied; weighs 7¼ lbs. Introduced 1996; still offered.

Perf.: $420   **Exc.:** $350   **VGood:** $280

Paul Goodwin photo

STURM RUGER MODEL 44 CARBINE

Semi-automatic; 44 Mag.; 4-shot tubular magazine; 18½-inch barrel; magazine release button incorporated in 1967; unchecked walnut pistol-grip carbine stock; barrel band; receiver tapped for scope mount; folding leaf rear sight, gold bead front. Introduced 1961; dropped 1985. Premium for 1961-1962 specimens marked "Deerstalker."

Exc.: $495 **VGood:** $380 **Good:** $300

Sturm Ruger Model 44 International

Same specs as Model 44 except full-length Mannlicher-type walnut stock; sling swivels. Dropped 1971.

Exc.: $795 **VGood:** $625 **Good:** $395

Sturm Ruger Model 44RS

Same specs as Model 44 except sling swivels; built-in peep sight.

Exc.: $480 **VGood:** $390 **Good:** $330

Sturm Ruger Model 44 Sporter

Same specs as Model 44 except sling swivels; Monte Carlo sporter stock; grooved forearm; grip cap; flat buttplate. Dropped 1971.

Exc.: $545 **VGood:** $450 **Good:** $380

Sturm, Ruger

STURM RUGER MODEL 77R

Bolt-action; 22-250, 220 Swift, 243 Win., 7mm-08, 6.5 Rem. Mag., 280 Rem., 284 Win., 308 Win., 300 Win. Mag., 338 Win. Mag., 350 Rem. Mag., 25-06, 257 Roberts, 250-3000, 6mm Rem., 270 Win., 7x57mm, 7mm Rem. Mag., 30-06; 3-, 5-shot magazine, depending upon caliber; 22-inch tapered barrel; hinged floorplate; adjustable trigger; hand-checkered American walnut stock; pistol-grip cap; sling swivel studs; recoil pad; integral scope mount base; optional folding leaf adjustable rear sight, gold bead ramp front. Introduced in 1968; no longer in production. Replaced by the Model M77 Mark II.

Perf.: $420 **Exc.:** $350 **VGood:** $320

350 Rem. Mag. caliber

Perf.: $470 **Exc.:** $390 **VGood:** $360

Sturm, Ruger

Sturm Ruger Model 77RL Ultra Light

Bolt-action; 243 Win., 308, 270, 30-06, 257, 22-250, 250-3000; 3-, 5-shot magazine, depending upon caliber; 20-inch light barrel; Sturm Ruger 1-inch scope rings. hinged floorplate; adjustable trigger; hand-checkered American walnut stock; pistol-grip cap; sling swivel studs; recoil pad; integral scope mount base; optional folding leaf adjustable rear sight, gold bead ramp front. Introduced in 1983; no longer in production.

Perf.: $420   **Exc.:** $350   **VGood:** $300

Sturm, Ruger

Sturm Ruger Model 77RS

Bolt-action; magnum-size action; 257 Roberts, 25-06, 270 Win., 30-06, 7mm Rem. Mag., 300 Win. Mag., 338 Win. Mag.; 3-, 5-shot, depending upon caliber; 22-inch barrel (270, 30-06, 7x57, 280 Rem.); 24-inch barrel (all others). Hinged floorplate; adjustable trigger; hand-checkered American walnut stock; pistol-grip cap; sling swivel studs; recoil pad; integral scope mount base; optional folding leaf adjustable rear sight, gold bead ramp front. Introduced in 1968; no longer in production.

Perf.: $510   **Exc.:** $450   **VGood:** $400

Sturm, Ruger

STURM RUGER MODEL 77RSI INTERNATIONAL

Bolt-action; 18½-inch barrel. Hinged floorplate; adjustable trigger; full-length Mannlicher-style stock; steel forend cap; loop-type sling swivels; open sights; Sturm Ruger steel scope rings; improved front sight; 22-250, 250-3000, 243, 308, 270, 30-06; weighs 7 lbs; 38⅜-inch overall length. Introduced 1986.

Perf.: $495   **Exc.:** $410   **VGood:** $350

Sturm, Ruger

STURM RUGER NO. 1B STANDARD SINGLE SHOT

Single-shot; 204 Ruger, 218 Bee, 22 Hornet, 22-250, 220 Swift, 243 Win., 223, 257 Roberts, 280, 6mm Rem., 25-06, 270 Win., 308, 30-06, 7mm Rem. Mag., 300 Win. Mag., 338 Mag., 270 Weatherby, 300 Weatherby; 26-inch barrel with quarter rib; American walnut, two-piece stock; hand-checkered pistol grip, forearm; open sights or integral scope mounts; hammerless falling-block design; automatic ejector; top-tang safety. Introduced 1967; still in production.

Perf.: $670   **Exc.:** $580   **VGood:** $385

Sturm, Ruger

STURM RUGER NO. 1A LIGHT SPORTER

Single-shot; 22-inch barrel; American walnut, two-piece stock; Alex Henry-style forearm; iron sights; 204 Ruger, 243 Win., 270 Win., 30-06, 7x57mm. Hammerless falling-block design; automatic ejector; top-tang safety. Introduced 1968; still in production.

Perf.: $665   **Exc.:** $580   **VGood:** $385

Sturm, Ruger

STURM RUGER NO. 1S MEDIUM SPORTER

Single-shot; 7mm Rem. Mag., 300 Win. Mag., 338 Win. Mag., 45-70; 26-inch barrel, 22-inch (45-70) barrel. American walnut, two-piece stock; Alex Henry-style forearm; iron sights. Hammerless falling-block design; automatic ejector; top-tang safety. Introduced 1968; still in production.

Perf.: $770   **Exc.:** $530   **VGood:** $420

Sturm, Ruger

STURM RUGER NO. 1H TROPICAL MODEL

Single-shot; 375 H&H Mag., 405 Win., 416 Rigby, 458 Win. Mag., 458 Lott; 24-inch heavy barrel; American walnut, two-piece stock; Alex Henry-style forearm; open sights. Hammerless falling-block design; automatic ejector; top-tang safety. Introduced 1968; still in production.

Perf.: $790 **Exc.:** $630 **VGood:** $470

Sturm, Ruger

STURM RUGER NO. 1RSI INTERNATIONAL

Single-shot; full-length Mannlicher-style stock of American walnut, 20-inch barrel; 243, 30-06, 7x57, 270. Hammerless falling-block design; automatic ejector; top-tang safety. Introduced 1983; still in production.

Perf.: $780 **Exc.:** $580 **VGood:** $410

Sturm, Ruger

STURM RUGER NO. 1V SPECIAL VARMINTER

Single-shot; 24-inch heavy barrel; 22-250, 220 Swift, 223, 25-06, 6mm; supplied with target scope bases. Hammerless falling-block design; automatic ejector; top-tang safety. Introduced 1970; still in production.

Perf.: $760   **Exc.:** $620   **VGood:** $475

Did You Know?

Sturm Ruger is currently the only U.S. manufacturer producing firearms in all four market divisions: rifles, shotguns, pistols, and revolvers.

THOMPSON/CENTER ARMS CO.

PO Box 5002
Rochester, NH 03866
Phone: *603-332-2394*
Website: *www.tcarms.com*

Thompson/Center is a young company, as things go in the U.S. firearms industry, but it has been a leader in identifying and developing important shooting sports categories.

The T/C Hawken rifle is the first successful commercial non-replica muzzleloader and helped launch the modern muzzleloading activity in this country, and around the world. The T/C Hawken remains in production today, the oldest non-replica muzzleloader on the market.

The other flagship of the T/C brand is the Contender single-shot pistol, introduced in 1967 and quickly embraced by handgun hunters and the handgun silhouette community.

The Contender's great appeal and enduring value is the pioneering interchangeable barrel system, and the wide array of cartridges for which it has been chambered. What a great system—buy one pistol, and add chamberings by simply buying additional barrels.

In a variety of barrel shapes (round tapered, round bull or octagon), materials (blued or stainless steel) and lengths, factory (and T/C Custom Shop) Contender barrels have been chambered for the following cartridges over the years:

Contender Chamberings

17 Mach2 Rimfire, 17 Hornady Mag Rimfire, 17 K-Hornet, 17 Ackley Bee, 17 Mach IV, 17 Remington, 204 Ruger, 22 Short Match, 22 Long Rifle, 22 Long Rifle w/Match Chamber, 22 Winchester Magnum, 22 Remington Jet, 22 Hornet, 22 K-Hornet, 218 Bee, 219 Zipper, 221 Fireball, 222 Remington, 222 Remington Magnum, 223 Remington, 223 Ackley Improved, 6mm T/C-U, 25-20 Winchester, 256 Winchester Magnum, 25-35 Winchester, 6.5mm T/C-U, 6.8mm Remington, 7-30 Waters, 7mm T/C-U, 300 Whisper, 30 M-1 Carbine, 30 Herrett, 30-30 Winchester, 30-30 Ackley Improved, 32-20 Winchester (w/.308-in. groove dia.), 32 H&R Magnum (w/.308-in. groove dia.), 9mm Luger (w/.357-in. groove dia.), 357-44 Bain & Davis, 38 Special, 357 Magnum, 357 Remington Maximum, 357 Herrett, 35 Remington, 38-55 Winchester, 375 Winchester, 375 JDJ, 41 Remington Magnum, 414 Super Mag, 445 Super Mag, 44 Remington Magnum, 45 ACP, 45 Colt, 45 Winchester Magnum, 45-70 Government and 45 Colt/.410 bore.

In December 2006, Smith & Wesson announced the purchase of Thompson/Center Arms.

Did You Know?

In 1965, Thompson/Center was formed by the union of K. W. Thompson Tool and gun designer, Warren Center.

Paul Goodwin photo

THOMPSON/CENTER CONTENDER

Single shot; break-open action; chambered for 29 calibers; 8¾-inch, 10-inch, 14-inch round, heavy, octagon barrel; adjustable sights; checkered walnut grip, forearm; interchangeable barrels; detachable choke for shot cartridges; blued finish. Introduced 1967; superceded by the G2 and Encore models.

New: $350   **Perf.:** $300   **Exc.:** $275

Thompson/Center Contender Bull Barrel Armour Alloy II

Same specs as Contender except chambered for 7 calibers; 10-inch round barrel; extra-hard satin finish. Introduced 1986; discontinued 1989.

Perf.: $300   **Exc.:** $250   **VGood:** $200

Thompson/Center Contender Stainless

Same specs as Contender except stainless steel construction with blued sights; black Rynite forend; ambidextrous finger-groove grip with built-in rubber recoil cushion with sealed-in air pocket; receiver with different cougar etching; 10-inch bull barrel in 22 LR, 22 LR Match, 22 Hornet, 223 Rem., 30-30 Win., 357 Mag., 44 Mag., 45 Colt/410. Made in U.S. by Thompson/Center. Introduced 1993.

New: $375   **Perf.:** $350   **Exc.:** $300

Thompson/Center Contender Vent Rib Barrel

Same specs as Contender except 357 Mag., 44 Mag., 45 Colt/410; 10-inch vent rib barrel.

Perf.: $400   **Exc.:** $350   **VGood:** $325

Thompson/Center Contender Vent Rib Barrel Armour Alloy II

Same specs as Contender except 45 Colt/410 only; 10-inch vent rib barrel; extra hard satin finish. Introduced 1986; dropped 1997.

Perf.: $350   **Exc.:** $300   **VGood:** $275

WINCHESTER REPEATING ARMS COMPANY

New Haven, Connecticut

Formed in New Haven, Connecticut, in 1866, the Winchester Repeating Arms Company developed the rimfire Henry Rifle, chambering an early rimfire cartridge. The Henry, suitably improved with a new magazine system, then became the Winchester Model 1866, chambered for an improved rimfire cartridge. The legendary Model 1873, chambered for the new 44-40 Winchester centerfire cartridge, followed in just a few years. The company prospered and newer, improved rifles and shotguns were introduced.

Work continued after World War I, creating the Model 52 (1920) rimfire bolt-action target rifle and the Model 54 (1925) and Model 70 (1936) bolt-action centerfire rifles. Winchester also made single-shot, slide-action and autoloading rimfire rifles; single-barrel, double-barrel, lever-action, slide-action and autoloading shotguns as well as the bolt-action, lever action, single-shot (into the 1930s) and autoloading centerfire rifles.

Collectors of a more purist bent may not look at a Winchester made after 1963, given the substantial changes made in much of the product from 1964 onward. However, the company did make good guns post-1964, and most represent excellent value for today's shooting sportsman.

The latter '60s may be regarded as a shaking-out period for the company's marketing philosophy, and the post-'64 product "improvements" began to disappear as protesting customers stayed away in droves. The pressed-in checkering disappeared, and the newly-introduced Monte Carlo stock design did not last very long, being superceded by the classic stock design in the latter '70s and early '80s as new models appeared. Finally, the pre-64 Model 70 bolt action was reintroduced on a number of the bolt-action rifles in 1994.

The company's Model 94 rifle and carbine were very big in the commemorative business from the mid-1960s to the latter '90s.

The company's modern heyday was quite likely the period between the 1930s and early 1960s. In recent years, the New Haven plant manufactured the Model 70 and Model 94 rifles and the Model 1300 shotgun.

However, all things change and the Winchester plant in New Haven closed its doors permanently in March, 2006, and the machinery was auctioned off.

The Winchester brand name still appears on rifles and shotguns manufactured overseas and marketed by Browning Arms/U.S. Repeating Arms, in Morgan, Utah. There are millions of U.S.-made Winchester firearms out there, and a visit to your local gunshop, gun show or newpaper classified section will almost certainly turn up a number of them. The older (pre-1900) Winchesters are firmly in the serious collector category, but the newer guns—with a few exceptions—are plentiful and still affordable to the average shooter & collector.

Did You Know?

Sarah L. Winchester, the heiress to the rifle manufacturing empire, was told that the Winchester family was cursed and haunted by the ghosts of people who were killed by Winchester rifles. She moved to San Jose, California, and built the Winchester Mystery House, a large and complex mansion supposedly designed to ward off these spirits.

Courtesy Dixie Gunworks

WINCHESTER MODEL 1890

Slide action; 22 Short, 22 Long, (not interchangeable), 22 WRF, (22 LR was added after 1919); 15-shot tube magazine (22 Short), 12-shot (22 Long), 11-shot (22 LR), 10-shot (22 WRF); 24-inch octagonal barrel; open rear, bead front sight; plain, straight stock, grooved slide handle; visible hammer; originally solid-frame design; after serial No. 15,552, all were takedowns; color case-hardened (pre-1901) or blued (post-1901) finish. Collector value. Because of production variations, expert appraisal is recommended. Introduced 1890; discontinued 1934.

Color case-hardened model
Exc.: $4500   **VGood:** $3600   **Good:** $2100

Blued finish
Exc.: $1495   **VGood:** $995   **Good:** $765

Courtesy Dixie Gunworks

WINCHESTER MODEL 1895

Lever action; 30-40 Krag, 30 Govt.'03 (30-03), 30 Govt.'06 (30-06), 303 British, 7.62mm Russian, 35 Win., 38-72, 405 Win., 40-72; 4-, 5-shot (30-40, 303 British) box magazine; 24-inch, 28-inch barrel; open rear sight, bead or blade front; uncheckered American walnut straight-grip stock, forend; blued finish. Introduced 1895; discontinued 1931. Collector value.

Exc.: $4000   **VGood:** $2500   **Good:** $1400

Takedown model
Exc.: $4400   **VGood:** $2800   **Good:** $1600

Winchester Model 1895 Carbine

Same specs as Model 1895 except 30-40 Krag, 30-03, 30-06, 303 British; 22-inch barrel; one barrel band; carbine stock; solid frame. Collector value.

Exc.: $2900   **VGood:** $2000   **Good:** $1000

With U.S. Government markings
Exc.: $4000   **VGood:** $3300   **Good:** $1800

Courtesy Dixie Gunworks

WINCHESTER MODEL 1903

Semi-automatic; 22 Winchester Automatic RF cartridge; 10-shot tube magazine in butt; 20-inch barrel; takedown; open rear sight, bead front; uncheckered straight-grip stock, forend; special wood and factory checkering bring a premium. Introduced 1903; discontinued 1932. Collector value.

Exc.: $785   **VGood:** $515   **Good:** $345

Deluxe rifle with checkered pistol-grip stock and forearm
Exc.: $1200   **VGood:** $730   **Good:** $560

Did You Know?

The Model 1903 was Winchester's first semi-automatic firearm, and also its first hammerless repeater.

Courtesy Dixie Gunworks

WINCHESTER MODEL 1907

Semi-automatic; 351 Win. Self-Loading; 5-, 10-shot box magazine; 20-inch barrel; takedown; open rear sight, bead front; uncheckered walnut pistol-grip stock, forend. Introduced 1907; discontinued 1957. Collector value.

  Exc.: $415   **VGood:** $330   **Good:** $265

Did You Know?

Not just a hunting rifle, the 1907 found an unusual market in WWI. Allied aviators used the rifles in cockpit-to-cockpit gun battles.

Paul Goodwin photo

WINCHESTER MODEL 52 (Early Production)

Bolt action; 22 Short, 22 LR; 5-shot box magazine; 28-inch barrel; folding leaf peep rear sight, blade front; scope bases; semi-military stock; pistol grip; grooves on forearm. Later versions had higher comb, semi-beavertail forearm; slow lock model was replaced in 1929 by speed lock. Last arms of this model bore serial numbers followed by the letter "A." Introduced 1919; discontinued 1937.

Exc.: $975   **VGood:** $715   **Good:** $625

Winchester Model 52 Sporter

Same specs as Model 52 except for 24-inch lightweight barrel; weighs 7¼ lbs.; Lyman No. 48F receiver sight, Redfield gold bead on hooded ramp at front; deluxe walnut sporting stock with cheekpiece; checkered forend, pistol grip; black forend tip; leather sling. Beware of fakes. Introduced 1934; discontinued 1958.

Exc.: $3500   **VGood:** $3000   **Good:** $1900

Paul Goodwin photo

WINCHESTER MODEL 52A

Bolt action; 22 Short, 22 LR; 5-shot box magazine; 28-inch barrel; folding leaf peep rear sight, blade front; scope bases; semi-military stock; pistol grip; grooves on forearm; speedlock action. Introduced 1929; discontinued 1939.

> **Exc.:** $975   **VGood:** $825   **Good:** $675

Winchester Model 52A Heavy Barrel

Same specs as Model 52A except 28-inch heavy barrel; Lyman 17G front sight. Discontinued 1939.

> **Exc.:** 1100   **VGood:** $900   **Good:** $700

Winchester Model 52A Sporter

Same specs as Model 52A except 24-inch lightweight barrel; Lyman No. 48 receiver sight, gold bead on hooded ramp front; deluxe walnut sporting stock, checkered; black forend tip; cheekpiece. Introduced 1937; discontinued 1939.

> **Exc.:** $4500   **VGood:** $4000   **Good:** $2500

Paul Goodwin photo

WINCHESTER MODEL 52B

Bolt action; 22 Short, 22 LR; 5-shot box magazine; 28-inch barrel; various sighting options; target or Marksman pistol-grip stock with high comb, beavertail forearm; round-top receiver; redesigned Model 52A action. Introduced 1940; discontinued 1947.

Exc.: $900   **VGood:** $720   **Good:** $585

Winchester Model 52B Bull Gun
Same specs as Model 52B except 28-inch extra-heavy barrel; Marksman pistol-grip stock; Vaver No. 35 Mielt extension receiver sight, Vaver WIIAT front.

Exc.: $1000   **VGood:** $820   **Good:** $695

Winchester Model 52B Heavy Barrel
Same specs as Model 52B except 28-inch heavy barrel; Lyman No. 48FH rear sight, Lyman No. 77 front.

Exc.: $1195   **VGood:** $900   **Good:** $600

Winchester Model 52B Sporter
Same specs as Model 52 except 5-shot detachable box magazine; 24-inch lightweight barrel; Lyman No. 48 receiver sight, gold bead on hooded ramp front; deluxe walnut sporting stock, checkered; black forend tip; cheekpiece; sling swivels; single shot adapter.

Exc.: $3500   **VGood:** $2900   **Good:** $2000

Winchester Model 52B Sporter (1993)
Same specs as Model 52B except no sights; drilled, tapped for scope mounting; remake of early Model 52 Sporter; Model 52C mechanism with stock configuration of the Model 52B; Micro-Motion trigger. Production limited to 6000 rifles. Introduced 1993; discontinued 1993.

Perf.: $650   **Exc.:** $575   **VGood:** $390

Paul Goodwin photo

WINCHESTER MODEL 52C

Bolt action; 22 Short, 22 LR; 5-, 10-shot box magazine; 28-inch barrel; various sighting systems; Marksman pistol-grip stock with high comb, beavertail forearm; Micro-Motion trigger; single shot adapter. Introduced 1947; discontinued 1961.

Exc.: $1125   **VGood:** $920   **Good:** $680

Winchester Model 52C Bull Gun
Same specs as Model 52C except 28-inch extra-heavy bull barrel; weighs 12 lbs.

Exc.: $1200   **VGood:** $1000   **Good:** $795

Winchester Model 52C Heavy Barrel
Same specs as Model 52C except 28-inch heavy barrel.

Exc.: $1120   **VGood:** $940   **Good:** $670

Winchester Model 52C Sporter
Same specs as Model 52C except 24-inch lightweight barrel; Lyman No. 48 receiver sight, gold bead on hooded ramp front; deluxe walnut sporting stock, checkered; black forend tip; cheekpiece; sling swivels; single shot adapter; Micro-Motion trigger.

Exc.: $3400   **VGood:** $2900   **Good:** $2000

Paul Goodwin photo

WINCHESTER MODEL 52D

Bolt action; single shot; 22 LR; 28-inch free-floating standard or heavy barrel; 46-inch overall length; weighs 9¾ lbs. (standard barrel), 11 lbs. (heavy barrel); no sights; scope blocks for standard target scopes; redesigned Marksman stock; rubber buttplate; accessory channel in stock with forend stop. Introduced 1961; discontinued 1980.

> **Exc.:** $1100   **VGood:** $920   **Good:** $750

Winchester Model 52D International Match

Same specs as Model 52D except laminated international-style stock with aluminum forend assembly; hook butt plate; adjustable palm rest; ISU or Kenyon trigger. Introduced 1969; discontinued 1980.

> *ISU trigger*
> **Exc.:** $1960   **Vgood:** $1850   **Good:** $1740
>
> *Kenyon trigger*
> **Exc.:** $2000   **VGood:** $1900   **Good:** $1800

Winchester Model 52D International Prone

Same specs as Model 52D International Match except stock designed for prone shooting only; no hook butt plate or palm rest; oil-finished stock with removable roll-over cheekpiece for easy bore cleaning. Introduced 1975; discontinued 1980.

> **Exc.:** $1000   **VGood:** $900   **Good:** $700

Paul Goodwin photo

WINCHESTER MODEL 53

Lever action; 25-20, 32-20, 44-40; 6-shot half-magazine; 22-inch barrel; open rear sight, bead front; walnut pistol-grip or straight-grip stock; blued finish; based on the Model 92 design. Introduced 1924; discontinued 1932.

Exc.: $2295 **VGood:** $1295 **Good:** $795

Takedown model
Exc.: $2495 **VGood:** $1495 **Good:** $995

(Premium for 44-40 Cal)

Did You Know?

The Model 53 was not a big seller for Winchester. It was revamped and reissued as the Winchester Model 65.

Paul Goodwin photo

WINCHESTER MODEL 54

Bolt action; 270, 7x57mm, 30-30, 30-06, 7.65x53mm, 9x57mm; 5-shot box magazine; 24-inch barrel; open rear sight, bead front; checkered pistol-grip stock; two-piece firing pin; steel buttplate (checkered from 1930 on). Introduced 1925; discontinued 1930.

    Exc.: $675   **VGood:** $575   **Good:** $425

Winchester Model 54 Carbine

Same specs as Model 54 except 20-inch barrel; plain pistol-grip stock; grooves on forearm. Introduced 1927; discontinued 1930.

    Exc.: $750   **VGood:** $675   **Good:** $450

Winchester Model 54 Improved

Same specs as Model 54 except with mechanical improvements; 22 Hornet, 220 Swift, 250-3000, 257 Roberts, 270, 7x57mm, 30-06; 24-inch, 26-inch (220 Swift) barrel; NRA-type stock; checkered pistol-grip, forearm; one-piece firing pin; speed lock. Introduced 1930; discontinued 1936.

    Exc.: $675   **VGood:** $600   **Good:** $445

Winchester Model 54 Improved Carbine

Same specs as Model 54 except 22 Hornet, 220 Swift, 250-3000, 257 Roberts, 270, 7x57mm, 30-06; 20-inch barrel; lightweight or NRA-type stock; checkered pistol-grip, forearm; one-piece firing pin; speed lock. Introduced 1930; discontinued 1936.

    Exc.: $700   **VGood:** $650   **Good:** $475

Paul Goodwin photo

WINCHESTER MODEL 55 CENTERFIRE

Lever action; 25-35, 30-30, 32 Spl.; 3-shot tubular magazine; 24-inch round barrel; open rear sight, bead front; uncheckered American walnut straight grip stock, forend. Based on Model 94 design. Collector value. Introduced 1924; discontinued 1932.

Exc.: $1495   **VGood:** $895   **Good:** $595

Takedown model
Exc.: $1595   **VGood:** $995   **Good:** $650

Did You Know?

The Model 55 was introduced after Winchester decided to discontinue all the variations of the Model 1894 rifle and continue to manufacture the rifle in only one standard model.

Paul Goodwin photo

WINCHESTER MODEL 55 RIMFIRE

Single shot, "semi-automatic;" 22 Short, 22 Long, 22 LR; 22-inch barrel; weighs 5½ lbs.; action automatically ejects the fired case, recocks, and remains open for loading after each shot; top loading; open rear sight, bead front; one-piece uncheckered walnut stock. Introduced 1958; discontinued 1961.

   Exc.: $210   **VGood:** $170   **Good:** $100

Did You Know?

The Model 55 Rimfire was
not numbered and approximately
47,000 were manufactured.

Paul Goodwin photo

WINCHESTER MODEL 57

Bolt action; 22 Short, 22 LR; 5-, 10-shot magazine; 22-inch barrel; Lyman peep sight, blade front; drilled, tapped receiver; semi-military-type pistol-grip target stock; swivels; web sling; barrel band. Introduced 1927; discontinued 1936. Premium for 22 Short chambering.

Exc.: $650   **VGood:** $495   **Good:** $385

Did You Know?

The Model 57 was too light and the barrel was too short to meet the requirements of a target rifle.

Courtesy Dixie Gunworks

WINCHESTER MODEL 60

Bolt action; single shot; 22 Short, 22 Long, 22 LR; 23-inch barrel (until 1933), 27-inch thereafter; open rear sight, blade front; uncheckered pistol-grip hardwood stock; buttplate; takedown; manual cocking. Introduced 1931; discontinued 1934.

Exc.: $325   **VGood:** $200   **Good:** $160

Winchester Model 60A

Same specs as Model 60 except 27-inch barrel; Lyman rear peep sight, square-top front; heavy semi-military target stock; web sling. Introduced 1933; discontinued 1939.

Exc.: $495   **VGood:** $295   **Good:** $200

Courtesy Dixie Gunworks

WINCHESTER MODEL 61

Slide action; 22 Short, 22 Long, 22 LR; 20-shot tube magazine (22 Short), 16-shot (22 Long), 14-shot (22 LR); 24-inch round or octagon barrel; hammerless; takedown; open rear sight, bead front; uncheckered pistol-grip stock; grooved semi-beavertail slide handle. Introduced 1932; discontinued 1963.

> **Exc.:** $650   **VGood:** $500   **Good:** $365
>
> *Octagon barrel model*
> **Exc.:** $1095   **VGood:** $795   **Good:** $495

Winchester Model 61 Magnum

Same specs as Model 61 except 22 WMR; 12-shot tube magazine. Introduced 1960; discontinued 1963.

> **Exc.:** $800   **VGood:** $650   **Good:** $525

Courtesy Dixie Gunworks

WINCHESTER MODEL 62

Slide action; 22 Short, 22 Long, 22 LR; 20-shot tube magazine (20 Short), 16-shot (22 Long), 14-shot (22 LR); 23-inch barrel; visible hammer; bead front sight, open rear; plain, straight-grip stock; grooved semi-beavertail slide handle; also available in gallery model in 22 Short only. Modernized version of Model 1890. Introduced 1932; discontinued 1959.

Exc.: $645   **VGood:** $465   **Good:** $350

Courtesy Dixie Gunworks

WINCHESTER MODEL 62A

Slide action; 22 Short, 22 Long, 22 LR; 20-shot tube magazine (20 Short), 16-shot (22 Long), 14-shot (22 LR); 23-inch barrel; visible hammer; bead front sight, open rear; plain, straight-grip stock; grooved semi-beavertail slide handle; also available in gallery model in 22 Short only. Similar to the Model 62, with minor changes. Introduced 1940 at serial no. 99,200; discontinued 1959.

Exc.: $645   **VGood:** $465   **Good:** $350

Paul Goodwin photo

WINCHESTER MODEL 63 (1933-1958)

Semi-automatic; 22 LR Super Speed or Super-X; 10-shot tube magazine in buttstock; 20-inch barrel (early series), 23-inch (later series); takedown; open rear sight, bead front; uncheckered walnut pistol-grip stock and forearm. Introduced 1933; discontinued 1958.

20-inch barrel
Exc.: $1350   **VGood:** $900   **Good:** $575

23-inch barrel
Exc.: $900   **VGood:** $720   **Good:** $520

Did You Know?

Model 63, the "improved Model 1903" was instrumental in the tremendous amount of sales for total production: close to 175,000!

Paul Goodwin photo

WINCHESTER MODEL 64 (Early Production)

Lever action; 219 Zipper, 25-35, 30-30, 32 Spl.; 20-inch, 24-inch barrel; weighs 7 lbs.; Winchester No. 22H open sporting or Lyman No. 56 (20-inch barrel) open rear sight, hooded ramp bead front; uncheckered American walnut pistol-grip stock, forend. Originally manufactured 1933 to 1957. Collector value on original production.

Exc.: $1295   **VGood:** $895   **Good:** $540

Winchester Model 64 Deer Rifle

Same specs as Model 64 except 30-30, 32 Spl.; weighs 7¾ lbs.; hand-checkered pistol-grip stock, forend; 1-inch sling swivels; sling; checkered steel buttplate; discontinued 1957.

Exc.: $1320   **VGood:** $950   **Good:** $650

Winchester Model 64 Zipper

Same specs as Model 64 except chambered for 219 Zipper; 26-inch barrel; weighs 7 lbs.; Winchester No. 98A peep rear sight. Introduced 1938; discontinued 1941. Collector value.

Exc.: $1695   **VGood:** $1295   **Good:** $995

Paul Goodwin photo

WINCHESTER MODEL 64 (Late Production)

Lever action; 30-30; 5-shot tube magazine; 24-inch barrel; open rear sight, ramped bead front; uncheckered American walnut pistol-grip stock, forend. Introduced 1972; discontinued 1973.

Exc.: $395   **VGood:** $300   **Good:** $250

Paul Goodwin photo

WINCHESTER MODEL 65

Lever action; 218 Bee, 25-20, 32-20; 7-shot tube half-magazine; 22-inch, 24-inch (218 Bee) barrel; based on the Model 92 design; weighs 6½ lbs.; open or peep rear sight, Lyman gold bead front on ramp base; plain pistol-grip stock, forearm; shotgun-type butt with checkered steel buttplate. Introduced 1933; discontinued 1947.

Exc.: $2795   **VGood:** $1995   **Good:** $1050

Courtesy Dixie Gunworks

WINCHESTER MODEL 67

Bolt action; single shot; 22 Short, 22 Long, 22 LR, 22 WMR, 22-shot cartridge; 24-inch rifled, 27-inch rifled or smoothbore barrel; takedown; open rear sight, bead front; uncheckered pistol-grip stock; grooved forearm (early models); manual cocking. Introduced 1934; discontinued 1963.

Exc.: $190   **VGood:** $150   **Good:** $125

Winchester Model 67 Junior (Boy's Rifle)
Same specs as Model 67 except 20-inch barrel; shorter stock.

Exc.: $240   **VGood:** $200   **Good:** $130

Did You Know?

In 1942, the Model 67s that were equipped with telescopes were taken off the market because of the war's demand for the telescopes.

Paul Goodwin photo

WINCHESTER MODEL 68

Bolt action; single shot; 22 Short, 22 Long, 22 LR, 22 WMR; 24-inch, 27-inch; takedown; adjustable rear peep sight, ramp front; uncheckered walnut pistol-grip stock; grooved forearm (early models); manual cocking. Introduced 1934; discontinued 1946.

Exc.: $285   **VGood:** $205   **Good:** $145

Did You Know?

The Model 68 had a more expensive sight so it sold for a higher price than the Model 67. As a result of this, fewer Model 68s were sold.

Paul Goodwin photos

WINCHESTER MODEL 69, 69A

Bolt action; 22 Short, 22 Long, 22 LR; 5-, 10-shot detachable box magazine; 25-inch barrel; takedown; open rear sight, bead ramp front; uncheckered pistol-grip stock. Introduced 1935; discontinued 1963.

Exc.: $315   **VGood:** $230   **Good:** $190

Winchester Model 69 Match

Same specs as Model 69 except Lyman No. 57EW receiver sight, Winchester No. 101 front; Army-type leather sling.

Exc.: $335   **VGood:** $245   **Good:** $210

Winchester Model 69 Target

Same specs as Model 69 except rear peep sight, Winchester No. 93 blade front sight; sling swivels; Army-type leather sling.

Exc.: $325   **VGood:** $240   **Good:** $200

WINCHESTER MODEL 70

This bolt action, centerfire repeating rifle is a versatile longarm, having been produced in more variations and configurations than any other of the manufacturer's firearms. The rifle is divided into roughly three historical categories, the original variations having been made from 1936 to 1963; at that time, the rifle was redesigned to a large degree, actually downgraded in an effort to meet rising costs, but to hold the retail price. This series of variations was produced from 1964 until 1972, at which time the rifle was upgraded and the retail price increased. Additional changes have been made in years since.

Paul Goodwin photo

WINCHESTER MODEL 70 (1936-1963)

Bolt action; 22 Hornet, 220 Swift, 243, 250-3000, 7mm, 257 Roberts, 264 Win. Mag., 270, 7x57mm, 300 Savage, 300 H&H Mag., 300 Win. Mag., 30-06, 308, 338 Win. Mag., 35 Rem., 358 Win., 375 H&H Mag., (other calibers on special order such as 9x57mm and 7.65mm); 4-shot box magazine (magnums); 5-shot (other calibers); 20-inch, 24-inch, 25-inch, 26-inch barrel; claw extractor; hooded ramp front sight, open rear; hand-checkered walnut pistol-grip stock; Monte Carlo comb on later productions. Introduced 1936; discontinued 1963. In many cases, the value depends largely on the caliber of the rifle. Note: 300 Savage, 35 Rem., 7.65mm, 9x57mm very rare; see appraiser.

Pre-WWII (1936-1945)

Standard calibers
Exc.: $1100   **VGood:** $850   **Good:** $650

220 Swift, 257 Roberts, 300 H&H Mag.
Exc.: $1400   **VGood:** $900   **Good:** $700

375 H&H Mag., 7x57mm, 250-3000
Exc.: $1800   **VGood:** $1100   **Good:** $900

WINCHESTER MODEL 70 *(cont.)*

Post-WWII (1946-1963)

Standard calibers
Exc.: $1000   **VGood:** $800   **Good:** $600

220 Swift, 243, 257 Roberts
Exc.: $1300   **VGood:** $900   **Good:** $650

22 Hornet, 300 H&H Mag.,
Exc.: $1700   **VGood:** $1300   **Good:** $1100

300 Win. Mag., 338 Win. Mag., 375 H&H Mag.
Exc.: $1700   **VGood:** $1200   **Good:** $1000
Note: 250-3000, 300 Savage, 358, 35 Rem., 7x57mm very rare; see appraiser.

Winchester Model 70 Alaskan
Same specs as Model 70 (1936-1963) except 300 Win. Mag., 338 Win. Mag., 375 H&H Mag.; 3-, 4-shot (375 H&H Mag.) magazine; 24-inch barrel (300 Win. Mag.), 25-inch barrel; 45⅝-inch overall length; weighs 8 to 8¾ lbs.; bead front, sight, folding leaf rear; tapped for scope mounts, receiver sights; Monte Carlo stock; recoil pad. Introduced 1960; discontinued 1963.
Exc.: $1900   **VGood:** $1400   **Good:** $995

Winchester Model 70 Bull Gun
Same specs as Model 70 (1936-1963) except 30-06, 300 H&H Mag.; 28-inch extra heavy barrel; scope bases; walnut target Marksman stock; Lyman No. 77 front sight, Lyman No. 48WH rear; Army-type leather sling strap. Discontinued 1963.
Exc.: $2300   **VGood:** $1700   **Good:** $1295

Winchester Model 70 Carbine
Same specs as Model 70 (1936-1963) except 22 Hornet, 250-3000, 257 Roberts, 270, 7x57mm, 30-06; 20-inch barrel. The 250-3000, 7x57mm are rare; see appraiser. Introduced 1936; discontinued 1946.

Calibers 270, 30-06
Exc.: $1695   **VGood:** $1195   **Good:** $895

22 Hornet, 257 Roberts
Exc.: $2695   **VGood:** $1995   **Good:** $1295

WINCHESTER MODEL 70 *(cont.)*

Winchester Model 70 Featherweight
Same specs as Model 70 (1936-1963) except 243, 264 Win. Mag., 270, 308, 30-06, 358 Win.; 22-inch lightweight barrel, 24-inch (special order); weighs 6½ lbs.; lightweight American walnut Monte Carlo or straight comb stock; checkered pistol grip, forend; aluminum triggerguard, checkered buttplate, floorplate; 1-inch swivels. Introduced 1952; discontinued 1963.

Calibers 243, 270, 30-06, 308
Exc.: $1050   **VGood:** $800   **Good:** $650

264 Win. Mag., 358 Win.
Exc.: $1600   **VGood:** $1300   **Good:** $1000

Super Grade
Same specs as Model 70 (1936-1963) except 24-inch, 25-inch, 26-inch barrel; Winchester 22G open sporting rear sight; deluxe stock, cheekpiece; black forearm tip; sling; quick-detachable sling swivels; grip cap. Introduced 1936; discontinued 1960.
Exc.: $1950   **VGood:** $1300   **Good:** $1000

375 H&H Mag.
Exc.: $3000   **VGood:** $2300   **Good:** $1600

Winchester Model 70 Super Grade African
Same specs as Model 70 (1936-1963) except 458 Win. Mag.; 3-shot magazine; 25-inch barrel; weighs 9½ lbs.; Monte Carlo checkered walnut pistol-grip stock; cheekpiece; recoil pad; stock crossbolts; front sling swivel stud mounted on barrel. Introduced 1956; discontinued 1963.
Exc.: $3700   **VGood:** $3000   **Good:** $2300

Winchester Model 70 Super Grade Featherweight
Same specs as Model 70 (1936-1963) except 243, 270, 30-06, 308; 22-inch barrel; lightweight deluxe Monte Carlo stock, cheekpiece; black pistol-grip cap, forearm tip; aluminum buttplate, triggerguard, floorplate; sling; quick-detachable swivels. Discontinued 1960.
Exc.: $3050   **VGood:** $1995   **Good:** $1095

Winchester Model 70 Target
Same specs as Model 70 (1936-1963) except 24-inch, 26-inch medium-weight barrel; scope bases; walnut target Marksman stock; Lyman No. 77 front sight, Lyman No. 48WH rear, Army-type leather sling strap.
Exc.: $1995   **VGood:** $1100   **Good:** $795

Paul Goodwin photo

WINCHESTER MODEL 70 (1964-1971)

Bolt action; 22-250, 222, 225, 243, 270, 308, 30-06, (standard calibers); 5-shot box magazine; 22-inch heavy barrel; 42½-inch overall length; weighs 7 lbs.; plunger-type extractor; hooded ramp front sight, adjustable open rear; checkered walnut Monte Carlo stock, cheekpiece; sling swivels. Introduced 1964; discontinued 1971.

Exc.: $395   **VGood:** $325   **Good:** $300

Winchester Model 70 African
Same specs as Model 70 (1964-1971) except 375 H&H Mag., 458 Win. Mag.; 22-inch barrel (375 H&H Mag.), 24-inch (458 Win. Mag.); 42½-inch overall length; weighs 8½ lbs.; special sights; hand-checkered Monte Carlo stock; ebony forearm tip; recoil pad; quick-detachable swivels; sling; twin crossbolts. Introduced 1964; discontinued 1971.

Perf.: $795   **Exc.:** $525   **VGood:** $450

Winchester Model 70 Deluxe
Same specs as Model 70 (1964-1971) except 243, 270 Win., 30-06, 300 Win. Mag.; 3-shot magazine (magnum), 5-shot (other calibers); 22-inch, 24-inch barrel (magnum); hand-checkered walnut Monte Carlo stock, forearm; ebony forearm tip; recoil pad (magnum). Introduced 1964; discontinued 1971.

Perf.: $550   **Exc.:** $300   **VGood:** $250

Winchester Model 70 Magnum
Same specs as Model 70 (1964-1971) except 264 Win. Mag., 7mm Rem. Mag., 300 H&H Mag., 300 Win. Mag., 338 Win. Mag., 375 H&H Mag.; 3-shot magazine; 24-inch barrel; 4-4½-inch overall length; weighs 7¼ lbs.

Perf.: $550   **Exc.:** $395   **VGood:** $260

Paul Goodwin photo

WINCHESTER MODEL 70 (1972-Present)

Bolt action; 22-250, 222, 25-06, 243, 270, 308, 30-06; 5-shot box magazine; 22-inch swaged, floating barrel; removable hooded ramp bead front sight, open rear; tapped for scope mounts; walnut Monte Carlo stock; cut checkering on pistol grip, forearm; forend tip; hinged floorplate; steel grip cap; sling swivels. Introduced 1972; discontinued 1980.

Perf.: $460   **Exc.:** $300   **VGood:** $220

Winchester Model 70 Classic Custom Grade

Same specs as Model 70 (1972 to present) except 270, 30-06, 7mm Rem. Mag., 300 Win. Mag., 338 Win. Mag.; 3-shot (magnum), 5-shot magazine; 24-inch, 26-inch barrel; fancy satin-finished walnut stock; hand-honed and fitted parts. Introduced 1990; discontinued 1994.

Perf.: $1350   **Exc.:** $995   **VGood:** $695

Winchester Model 70 Classic Custom Grade Featherweight

Same specs as Model 70 (1972 to present) except 22-250, 223, 243, 270, 280, 30-06, 308, 7mm-08 Rem.; no sights; checkered, satin-finished, high-grade American walnut stock, Schnabel forend; rubber buttpad; high polish blued finish; controlled round feeding. Introduced 1992; no longer in production.

Perf.: $950   **Exc.:** $650   **VGood:** $500

Winchester Model 70 Classic Featherweight

Same specs as Model 70 (1972 to present) except 22-250, 223, 243, 270, 280, 30-06, 308, 7mm-08; no sights; scope bases and rings; standard-grade walnut stock; claw extractor; controlled-round feeding system. Introduced 1992; no longer in production.

Perf.: $590   **Exc.:** $510   **VGood:** $330

Winchester Model 70 Classic Sporter

Same specs as Model 70 (1972 to present) except 25-06, 264 Win. Mag., 270, 270 Win. Mag., 30-06, 300 Win. Mag., 300 Weatherby Mag., 338 Win. Mag., 7mm Rem. Mag.; 3-shot magazine (magnum), 5-shot (others); 24-inch, 26-inch barrel; controlled round feeding. Introduced 1994; no longer in production.

Perf.: $505   **Exc.:** $410   **VGood:** $360

Paul Goodwin photo

WINCHESTER MODEL 71

Lever-action; 348 Win.; 4-shot tube magazine; 24-inch barrel; weighs 8 lbs.; open rear sight, bead front on ramp with hood; plain walnut pistol-grip stock, beavertail forend; blued finish; action is improved version of Model 1886. Introduced 1936; discontinued 1957.

Exc.: $1000   **VGood:** $795   **Good:** $725

Winchester Model 71 Carbine

Same specs as Model 71 except 20-inch barrel. Introduced 1936; discontinued 1938.

Exc.: $2200   **VGood:** $1750   **Good:** $1350

Winchester Model 71 Deluxe

Same specs as Model 71 except No. 98A rear peep sight; checkered stock, forearm, grip cap; quick-detachable sling swivels; leather sling.

Exc.: $1795   **VGood:** $995   **Good:** $750

Courtesy Dixie Gunworks

WINCHESTER MODEL 74

Semi-automatic; 22 Short or 22 LR; 20-shot tube magazine in buttstock (22 Short), 14-shot (22 LR); 24-inch barrel; takedown; open rear sight, bead front; uncheckered one-piece pistol-grip stock; safety on top of receiver. Introduced 1939; discontinued 1955. Premium for 22 Short (Gallery) model.

Exc.: $295 **VGood:** $195 **Good:** $180

Did You Know?

The first delivery of a Model 74 to warehouse stock was made on February 15, 1939, in 22 Short chambering only.

Paul Goodwin photo

WINCHESTER MODEL 75 SPORTER

Bolt action; 22 LR; 5-, 10-shot clip magazine; 24-inch barrel; weighs 5½ lbs.; open rear sight, hooded ramp blade front; checkered select walnut stock, pistol grip; hard rubber grip cap; swivels; checkered steel buttplate; cocked with opening movement of bolt. Introduced 1939; discontinued 1958.

Exc.: $750   **VGood:** $625   **Good:** $525

Courtesy Dixie Gunworks

WINCHESTER MODEL 75 TARGET

Bolt action; 22 LR; 5-, 10-shot clip magazine; 28-inch barrel; 44¾-inch overall length; weighs 8⅝ lbs.; target scope or variety of sights; uncheckered walnut stock, semi-beavertail forearm, pistol grip; checkered steel buttplate; cocked with opening movement of bolt; 1-inch Army-type leather sling. Introduced 1938; discontinued 1958.

Exc.: $570   **VGood:** $440   **Good:** $300

Did You Know?

The Model 75 Target was equipped with a special combination of sights. The U.S. Goverment used these for training troops during World War II.

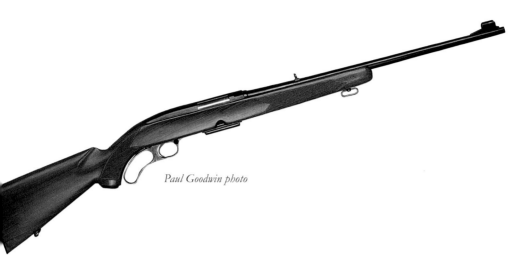

Paul Goodwin photo

WINCHESTER MODEL 88

Lever action; 243 Win., 284 Win., 308 Win., 358 Win.; 5-shot detachable box magazine; 22-inch barrel; 39½-inch overall length; weighs 6½ lbs.; hammerless; hooded white metal bead front sight, Lyman folding leaf middle sight; one-piece checkered walnut stock with steel-capped pistol grip, fluted comb, sling swivels; three-lug bolt; crossbolt safety; side ejection. Introduced 1955; discontinued 1974. Add 10% for 358.

308 Win.
Exc.: $495   **VGood:** $450   **Good:** $390

243 Win. (pre-1964)
Exc.: $615   **VGood:** $500   **Good:** $410

243 Win. (post-1964)
Exc.: $495   **VGood:** $450   **Good:** $390

284 Win. (pre-1964)
Exc.: $875   **VGood:** $650   **Good:** $550

284 Win. (post-1964)
Exc.: $650   **VGood:** $495   **Good:** $430

358 Win.
Exc.: $1250   **VGood:** $920   **Good:** $740

Winchester Model 88 Carbine
Same specs as Model 88 except 243, 284, 308; 19-inch barrel; barrel band. Introduced 1968; discontinued 1973.
Perf.: $1200   **Exc.:** $1090   **VGood:** $710

Paul Goodwin photo

WINCHESTER MODEL 94 (Post-1964 Production)

Lever action; 30-30, 25-35, 32 Spl., 7-30 Waters, 44 Mag.; 6-tube magazine; 20-inch, 24-inch barrel; weighs 6¼ lbs.; open rear sight, ramp front; plain American walnut straight-grip stock; barrel band on forearm; saddle ring; side or angle ejection (post-1982); blued finish. Introduced 1964; modified variations no longer in production.

> **Exc.:** $240　　　　**VGood:** $180　　　　**Good:** $150

> *Side or Angle Eject Model*
> **Exc.:** $250　　　　**VGood:** $195　　　　**Good:** $160

Winchester Model 94 Antique

Same specs as Model 94 except 20-inch barrel; case-hardened receiver with scrollwork; gold-colored saddle ring. Introduced 1964; discontinued 1983.

> **Exc.:** $230　　　　**VGood:** $200　　　　**Good:** $180

Winchester Model 94 Classic

Same specs as Model 94 except 30-30; 20-inch, 26-inch octagonal barrel; semi-fancy American walnut stock, forearm; steel buttplate; scrollwork on receiver. Introduced 1967; discontinued 1970.

> **Exc.:** $310　　　　**VGood:** $250　　　　**Good:** $200

Winchester Model 94 Trapper

Same specs as Model 94 except short 16-inch barrel; 30-30 (standard), 357 Mag., 44 Mag./44 Spl., 45 Colt; 5-shot tube magazine in 30-30, 9 shots in other calibers; side ejection. Introduced 1985; no longer in production.

> **Perf.:** $350　　　　**Exc.:** $240　　　　**VGood:** $200

Winchester Model 94 Deluxe

Same specs as Model 94 except 30-30; checkered walnut stock, forearm. Introduced 1988; later in production as Model 94 Traditional.

> **Exc.:** $250　　　　**VGood:** $205　　　　**Good:** $180

Courtesy Dixie Gunworks

Winchester Model 94 XTR
Same specs as Model 94 except higher-grade version; 30-30, 7-30 Waters; 20-inch, 24-inch barrel (7-30 Waters); hooded front sight; select checkered walnut straight-grip stock. Introduced 1978; discontinued 1988.

Exc.: $300   **VGood:** $275   **Good:** $250

7-30 Waters
Exc.: $400   **VGood:** $350   **Good:** $275

Winchester Model 94 XTR Big Bore *(shown)*
Same specs as Model 94 XTR except 307 Win., 356 Win., 375 Win.; 6-shot tube magazine; 20-inch barrel; cut-checkered satin-finish American walnut stock, rubber recoil pad. XTR designation dropped 1989. Introduced 1978.

Exc.: $400   **VGood:** $300   **Good:** $275

Side or Angle Eject model
Exc.: $425   **VGood:** $350   **Good:** $295

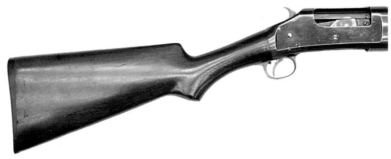

Courtesy Dixie Gunworks

WINCHESTER MODEL 1897

Slide action; visible hammer; takedown or solid frame; 12-, 16-ga.; 2¾-inch chamber; 5-shot tube magazine; 26-inch, 28-inch, 30-inch, 32-inch (12-ga. only) barrel; Full, Modified, Cylinder bore; intermediate chokes added 1931; uncheckered walnut half-pistol-grip stock, grooved forend. Introduced 1897; discontinued 1957.

Exc.: $600   **VGood:** $500   **Good:** $435

Winchester Model 1897 Brush

Same specs as Model 1897 except 26-inch Cylinder bore barrel. Introduced 1897; discontinued 1931.

Exc.: $425   **VGood:** $300   **Good:** $235

Winchester Model 1897 Special Trap

Same specs as Model 1897 except checkered fancy walnut trap-style stock, standard or beavertail forearm; engraving. Introduced 1931; discontinued 1939.

Exc.: $3500   **VGood:** $2250   **Good:** $1800

Winchester Model 1897 Standard Trap

Same specs as Model 1897 except Trap-style stock; replaced Model 1897 Trap. Introduced 1931; discontinued 1939.

Exc.: $800   **VGood:** $600   **Good:** $500

Winchester Model 1897 Trench

Same specs as Model 1897 except ventilated steel handguard; bayonet stud; built for U.S. Army during WWI. Introduced 1920; discontinued 1935.

Exc.: $2500   **VGood:** $1500   **Good:** $1300

Paul Goodwin photo

WINCHESTER MODEL 12

Slide action; hammerless; 12-, 16-, 20-, 28-ga.; 2¾-inch, 3-inch chamber; 5-shot magazine; 26-inch, 28-inch, 30-inch, 32-inch barrel; Improved Cylinder, Modified, Full choke; optional matted or vent rib; uncheckered walnut pistol-grip stock, forearm; blued. Introduced 1912; discontinued 1963.

With plain barrel
Exc.: $375   **VGood:** $280   **Good:** $225

With matted rib
Exc.: $450   **VGood:** $350   **Good:** $300

With vent rib
Exc.: $500   **VGood:** $400   **Good:** $350

Winchester Model 12 Featherweight

Same specs as Model 12 except 12-ga.; 26-inch Improved Cylinder, 28-inch Modified or Full, 30-inch Full barrel; alloy guard. Introduced 1959; discontinued 1962.
Exc.: $395   **VGood:** $325   **Good:** $290

Winchester Model 12 Heavy Duck

Same specs as Model 12 except 12-ga.; 3-inch chamber; 3-shot magazine; 30-inch, 32-inch Full barrel; plain, matted or vent rib; recoil pad. Introduced 1937; discontinued 1963.

With plain barrel
Exc.: $500   **VGood:** $350   **Good:** $300

With matted rib
Exc.: $625   **VGood:** $475   **Good:** $500

With vent rib
Exc.: $1000   **VGood:** $800   **Good:** $650

Winchester Model 12 Pigeon

Same specs as Model 12 except hand-checkered fancy walnut stock, forearm; engine-turned bolt, carrier; hand-worked action; optional carving and engraving. Introduced 1912; discontinued 1963.

Standard model with plain barrel
Exc.: $1250   **VGood:** $800   **Good:** $700

Standard model with vent rib
Exc.: $1375   **VGood:** $950   **Good:** $800

Winchester Model 12 Pigeon *(cont.)*

Skeet model with plain barrel
Exc.: $1250　　　　**VGood:** $800　　　　**Good:** $700

Skeet model with plain barrel, Cutts Compensator
Exc.: $1000　　　　**VGood:** $600　　　　**Good:** $500

Skeet model with vent rib
Exc.: $1250　　　　**VGood:** $950　　　　**Good:** $800

Trap model with matted rib
Exc.: $1200　　　　**VGood:** $900　　　　**Good:** $800

Trap model with vent rib
Exc.: $1250　　　　**VGood:** $950　　　　**Good:** $850

Winchester Model 12 Riot

Same specs as Model 12 except 12-ga.; 20-inch Cylinder barrel; vent handguard. Introduced 1918; discontinued 1963.

Military Version
Exc.: $850　　　　**VGood:** $600　　　　**Good:** $500

Civilian Version
Exc.: $450　　　　**VGood:** $375　　　　**Good:** $275

Winchester Model 12 Skeet

Same specs as Model 12 except 26-inch Skeet barrel; plain barrel or vent rib; red or ivory bead front sight; 94B middle; checkered walnut pistol-grip stock, extension slide handle; recoil pad. Introduced 1937; discontinued 1963.

With plain barrel
Exc.: $625　　　　**VGood:** $575　　　　**Good:** $500

With plain barrel, Cutts Compensator
Exc.: $475　　　　**VGood:** $375　　　　**Good:** $300

With vent rib
Exc.: $825　　　　**VGood:** $775　　　　**Good:** $700

Winchester Model 12 Trap

Same specs as Model 12 except 12-ga.; 30-inch Full-choke barrel; vent or matted rib; checkered walnut pistol-grip stock, extension slide handle; optional Monte Carlo stock; recoil pad. Introduced 1937; discontinued 1963.

With matted rib
Exc.: $700　　　　**VGood:** $500　　　　**Good:** $425

With vent rib
Exc.: $850　　　　**VGood:** $650　　　　**Good:** $575

With vent rib, Monte Carlo stock
Exc.: $975　　　　**VGood:** $775　　　　**Good:** $725

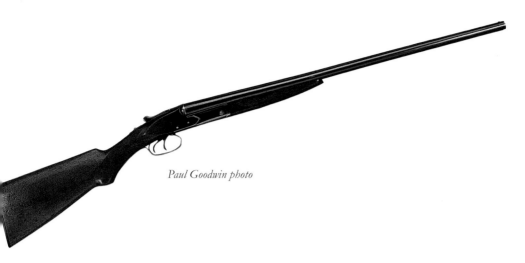

Paul Goodwin photo

WINCHESTER MODEL 21

Side-by-side; boxlock; hammerless; 12-, 16-, 20-, 28-ga., .410; 20-inch, 28-inch, 30-inch, 32-inch (12-ga. only) barrels; raised matted or vent rib; Full, Improved Modified, Modified, Improved Cylinder, Skeet chokes; checkered walnut straight or pistol-grip stock, regular or beavertail forend; automatic safety; early models (1931-1944) have double triggers and extractors, single trigger and ejectors optional; later models (1945-1959) have selective single trigger and selective ejectors. Introduced 1931; discontinued 1959.

With double triggers, extractors
Exc.: $1700   **VGood:** $1100   **Good:** $800

With double triggers, selective ejectors
Exc.: $2200   **VGood:** $1700   **Good:** $1450

With single selective trigger, extractors
Exc.: $1900   **VGood:** $1400   **Good:** $1100

With single selective trigger, selective ejectors
Exc.: $2500   **VGood:** $2000   **Good:** $1750

.410 model
Exc.: $30,000   **VGood:** $20,000   **Good:** $14,000

28-ga. model
Exc.: $20,000   **VGood:** $14,000   **Good:** $9000

Winchester Model 21 Duck

Same specs as Model 21 except 12-ga.; 3-inch chamber; 30-inch, 32-inch barrels; Full choke; checkered walnut pistol-grip stock, beavertail forearm; selective ejection; selective single trigger; recoil pad. Introduced 1940; discontinued 1954.

With matted rib
Exc.: $2500   **VGood:** $2000   **Good:** $1750

With vent rib
Exc.: $2800   **VGood:** $2300   **Good:** $2000

Winchester Model 21 Grand American

Same specs as Model 21 except two barrel sets; hand-checkered fancy American walnut stock, forearm; hand-honed internal parts; optional carving, engraving and gold inlays. Introduced 1960; discontinued 1982.

Perf.: $19,750   **Exc.:** $18,000   **VGood:** $15,000

Winchester Model 21 Skeet

Same specs as Model 21 except 26-inch, 28-inch barrels; Skeet chokes; red bead front sight; checkered French walnut stock, beavertail forearm; selective single trigger, selective ejection; non-auto safety. Introduced 1933; discontinued 1958.

With matted rib
Exc.: $1900   **VGood:** $1600   **Good:** $1300

With vent rib
Exc.: $2100   **VGood:** $1800   **Good:** $1500

Winchester Model 21 Trap

Same specs as Model 21 except 30-inch, 32-inch barrels; Full choke; checkered walnut pistol-grip or straight stock, beavertail forearm; selective trigger; non-auto safety; selective ejection. Introduced 1932; discontinued 1940.

With matted rib
Exc.: $1900   **VGood:** $1600   **Good:** $1300

With vent rib
Exc.: $2100   **VGood:** $1800   **Good:** $1500

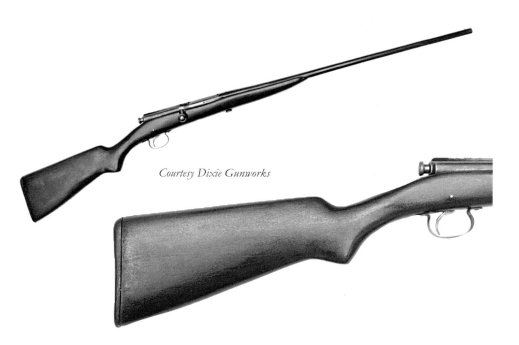

Courtesy Dixie Gunworks

WINCHESTER MODEL 41

Single shot; bolt action; takedown; .410; 2½-inch (pre-1933), 3-inch (post-1933) chamber; 24-inch full-choke barrel; uncheckered one-piece walnut pistol-grip or straight-grip stock; checkering on special order; guns were not numbered serially. Introduced 1920; discontinued 1934.

Exc.: $400 **VGood:** $300 **Good:** $250

Did You Know?

The Model 41 was the first shotgun of its type made in this country.

Courtesy Dixie Gunworks

WINCHESTER MODEL 50

Autoloader; 12-, 20-ga.; 2-shot magazine; 28-inch, 30-inch barrel; Improved, Modified, Full chokes; optional vent rib; 7¼ lbs.; bead-front sight; hand-checkered American walnut stock; fluted comb; composition buttplate; side ejection; short recoil action; interchangeable barrels. Introduced 1954; discontinued 1961.

> **Exc.:** $500   **VGood:** $450   **Good:** $390
>
> *With vent rib*
> **Exc.:** $540   **VGood:** $475   **Good:** $420

Winchester Model 50 Pigeon

Same specs as Model 50 except best-grade wood, carving and engraving. Introduced 1954; discontinued 1961.

> *Standard model*
> **Exc.:** $1000   **VGood:** $825   **Good:** $650
>
> *Featherweight model*
> **Exc.:** $1100   **VGood:** $800   **Good:** $600
>
> *Skeet model*
> **Exc.:** $1100   **VGood:** $900   **Good:** $750
>
> *Trap model*
> **Exc.:** $1100   **VGood:** $900   **Good:** $750

Winchester Model 50 Skeet

Same specs as Model 50 except 12-ga.; 26-inch vent-rib barrel; Skeet choke; hand-checkered American walnut Skeet-style stock. Introduced 1954; discontinued 1961.

> **Exc.:** $600   **VGood:** $525   **Good:** $420

Winchester Model 50 Trap

Same specs as Model 50 except 12-ga.; 30-inch vent-rib barrel; Full choke; hand-checkered American walnut Monte Carlo stock. Introduced 1954; discontinued 1961.

> **Exc.:** $600   **VGood:** $525   **Good:** $420